Alan Biggins
with contributions by Alice Biggins

30 Great Days Out in
Brittany

Kirkdale Books

Published by Kirkdale Books, Great Horwood, Buckinghamshire, MK17 0QQ

Printing history. First printed: February 2007

ISBN:978-0-9523149-7-4

Printed in Great Britain by Target Print, Leeds

British Library Cataloguing in publication data: A catalogue record is available for this book from the British Library,

Cover: Toulinguet Point (day 18), by H. Marcou, CRTB

My thanks to:
    Sue Mead & Paul Doodson for their excellent work on cover design
    Carol Farley, Hugh Brune and the staff at Portfolio, for keeping me on the straight and narrow
    The regional tourist board of Brittany, for permission to use their photographs
    John Whitehead, for help with maps and design.

I dedicate this book to Cora Knight. Too fast your evening fell.

Dear Reader,

In planning and writing this book, I have aimed to provide clear answers to those eternal travellers' questions – what, where, when, why, how, and how much. I have also tried to make it readable and easy to use. To meet these goals, you will notice that I have structured it slightly differently than a conventional guide book….

Rather than being an alphabetic list of towns, the book is based on and driven by maps. By looking at the map of Brittany on the next page, you should see at a glance several days-out near you. Each day then has one or more maps pinpointing enjoyable things to do – which are described in detail.

Where there are admission charges and opening times, I give them next to the attraction. I do not list phone numbers with attractions, but web site and email addresses, and post codes. This is because I doubt whether one in ten thousand non-French readers ever phone a French attraction, while most use the web and many use online mapping.

And I generally put tourist office addresses and opening times at the start of a town walk. You don't need to visit the offices to use the book, but it's a good idea to do so if they're open. French Tourist Offices are almost invariably well situated, and their staff are friendly, helpful, knowledgeable and multi-lingual. More importantly, perhaps, they generally supply free maps of a standard and size that a guide book, however large, cannot possibly recreate. They often provide other services, too, such as ferry bookings: and they always know exactly what is happening in the way of festivals and so on in their local area.

Finally, my web site, www.enhancefrance.com, is there to provide further information on France. I shall continue to improve and extend it. I appreciate feedback, and always seek to improve: don't hesitate to contact me via the site if you have any comments or suggestions.

I hope that you enjoy your visit.

Alan Biggins

Contents

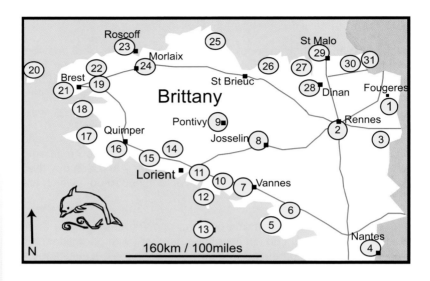

1. Fougères and Area

The Fortress in the East

1.1 The Town of Fougères

Population 23,000. Market days, Thursday 8am to 2pm and Saturday mornings.

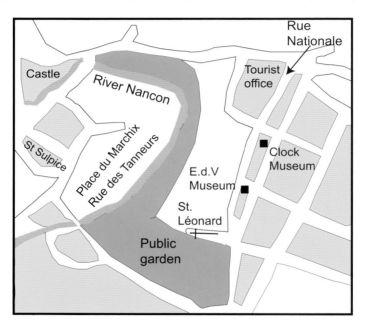

Fougères owes its foundation to the ridge upon which stands its castle, a vital fortress which dominates the Breton-Norman border. The old town grew up around the base of the castle and the church of Saint-Sulpice. The 'new' town, across the river, grew around the church of Saint-Léonard. The town's history has inspired many prominent authors. The town has 10 hotels, 25 restaurants, supermarkets and numerous shops.

It is advisable to visit the **Tourist Office** at 2 Rue Nationale, 35300, first (in July and August, a branch is also open in the castle), as they give good town maps and guides in English, which will further enhance your visit. They also sell several footpath guides – in French – for 2€ to 3€.

> **Open:** July and August, Mon to Sat, 9am to 7pm, Sun and bank holidays, 10am to noon, 2pm to 4pm. Rest of season (Easter to end October), it is closed on Monday mornings and between 12.30pm and 2pm every day. **Website:** www.ot-fougeres.fr (with an excellent map and partly English version). **Email:** ot.fougeres@wanadoo.fr

There is a **little train** that goes round the town, through the medieval quarter, the upper town and the public gardens. With a commentary in French and English.

E. de la Villeon museum
Ville de Fougeres/CRTB

The **Rue Nationale** houses the **Emmanuel de la Villeon museum** (he was an impressionist painter, entry is free) and a **Clock museum**.

Both close for lunch between 12pm and 2pm. The entry charge for the clock museum is: Adults - 4.50€. Child (10 to 18) - 3.70€. Under 10's – free. This pleasant pedestrianised street leads to the **Jardin Public**, a lovely garden with splendid views of the castle.

On the castle side of the river, the **Place du Marchix** and the medieval quarter still have some ancient houses. These half timbered buildings date back to the 17th century. **Rue des Tanneurs**

(Tanners' Street) evokes memories of one of the oldest activities of Fougères, facilitated by the quality of the water from the river Nançon - which also powered several mills. Here too is the church of **St-Sulpice**, much as it was in the 18th century. It has two notable granite altar pieces: that of the chapel of the tanners (beginning of the 15th century) and that of Notre-Dame (end of the 15th century). The choir, with its woodwork and wooden statues and altar, is a fine example of 18th century religious art.

Photo: Ville de Fougeres, CRTB

The breathtaking thing about Fougères, however, is its **Château** and town walls, for this castle is one of the most spectacular in Europe and in one of the best settings. Fortified since the eleventh century, the castle was built on a rocky outcrop above a river and a marsh. Many times besieged, slighted and rebuilt, Fougères was for centuries one of the key strongholds of Brittany.

Open: July and August, 9am to 7pm. Rest of year, 10am to noon, 2pm to 5pm. Closed January.
Cost: Adult - 4.80€. Child (10 to 16) - 2.20€. Under 10 - free.

The 13 towers of various ages, and a curtain wall, make this one of the most original, interesting and complete examples of medieval military architecture.

The castle is superbly sited in a bend of the river, with the town's ramparts connected to it. Entry to the chateau is through the advanced walls, a great rectangle guarded by three towers. There is a courtyard, then a moat, then the remains of the massive **De Coëtlogon Tower**, through which lies the main part of the castle. At the other end of the castle lies the last redoubt, where the keep (ruins) is flanked by the two highest towers. **The Gobelin Tower** was begun in the eleventh century and heightened in the fifteenth. The cylindrical **Mélusine Tower** is one of the greatest military works of the 14th century. Good views, both of the defences and the town, can be had from this tower. Beneath it there is a deep dungeon (oubliette, the French word, means 'forgotten'), from which escape was impossible.

Jutting out behind the castle, the back entrance, the postern gate, with its drawbridge, stood guard above the one-time river - now filled in to make a road to Rennes.

A Little History

Around the year 1000, the Duke of Brittany had a castle constructed to protect against the incursions of French and Norman raiders into Brittany. The lord of the manor sailed with William the Conqueror against England in 1066 and was granted part of the plunder, both in England and in Normandy. When the Norman kings of England attacked Brittany, the lord (Raoul) of Fougères resisted Henry II's attacks. The castle fell, only to be rebuilt by Raoul, being a key piece in the battle between England and France over who was going to annex Brittany.

One of the dukes of these years was Hugues de Lusignan, who traced his origins back to the fairy Mélusine. At this time, during the 13th century, many of the castle's grand towers were built.

Fougères and Area

As an example of the three-way struggle for Brittany, the castle was sacked in 1449 by the English, who defeated the French garrison, and massacred most of the inhabitants. The English were subsequently besieged by the Count of Brittany, plague broke out and the leader of the English troops surrendered. In 1488 the French took the castle again. At this point Fougères became definitively French, even before the rest of Brittany, and the castle lost its military significance, but became a gift of the French kings. Breton independence was still an issue in the eighteenth century. The American Revolution, which did so much to cause the French Revolution, was supported by (among others!) the local noble, the Marquis de la Rouërie, who, after covering himself in glory fighting alongside the American rebels, supported Breton independence on his return to France. For this he was imprisoned (he died in hiding, but that did not stop him being decapitated for treason afterwards). At this time arose the Chouan resistance to the revolution (their name comes from 'chou' which means owl, after the owl screech they used as a call). This peasant, Catholic army, founded in the Vendee, arose against the republic. They took, lost, and retook Fougères in a bloody series of battles which left many dead. Ambushes, slaughter, treachery and revenge left a legacy for many years afterwards.

In the nineteenth century this breathtaking, overgrown and romantic spot with its echoes of old glory became the haunt of artists and writers, being visited by such giants of French literature as Chateaubriand, Hugo and Balzac. In 1944 the final (to date) military chapter in the history of Fougères was written, when 300 inhabitants died in air raids and half of the houses were damaged or destroyed.

1.2 The Forest of Fougères

The forest of Fougères, immediately to the north of the town, covers about six square miles. It consists of beautiful beech and oak woods and is crisscrossed by trails. In the Forest, south of Landéan. on the right of the D177 road, just beyond the Chennedet crossroads, there is a fine Neolithic row of quartz blocks – the **Cordon des Druides**.

The stones run for some 250m (820ft), with 23 large blocks 1 metre high and many smaller. The forest of Fougères is full of mystery and legend and has walks to suit any level of fitness with easy colour-coded trails. There is a lakeside beach at **Chennedet**.

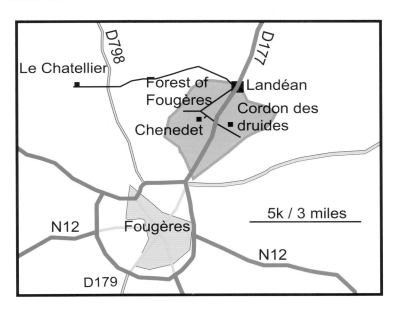

1.3 Floral Park of Haute-Bretagne

There is a botanical garden at **Le Chatellier**, 10 km north west of Fougères. It has lawns, lakes and 16 different garden areas (for example, the secret garden, the bamboo garden and the rose garden). The park has a shop and a tea shop.

Open: July and August, 10.30am to 6.30pm.
April, May, June, September, 10am to noon, 2pm to 6pm.
March, Oct & Nov, 2pm until 5.30pm. Closed mid November until March.
Cost: Adult - 8.90€. Aged 13 to 18 - 7.30€. Aged 4 to 12 – 6.30€.
Website: www.parcfloralbretagne.com (has English translation).

Rennes and Area

2. Rennes and Area

The Capital

2.1 A Walk around Rennes

Population 212,000

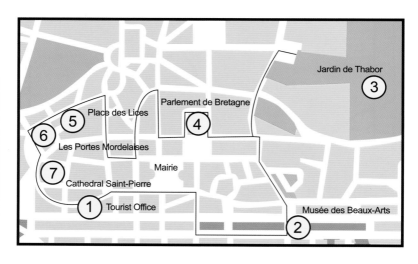

Rennes, the capital of Brittany, is a lively and very interesting city, well worth walking around. Should you be considering a longer stay here, a good place to start is the **Tourist Office (1)**, 11 Rue St Yves, 35000. This is to pick up maps and brochures of the town.

Rennes is quite outstanding in the quality of its handouts, offering fine free guides in English. Look out especially for 'let us tell you the story of Rennes' which has a map with no less than 53 points of interest, each illustrated and explained – a master guide for a fine city walk. Also enquire here If you wish to visit the Parliament of Brittany (guided tour, in French, see below).

Open: 1st April to 30th September, daily, from 9am to 7pm (11am to 6pm on Sundays and public holidays). During the rest of the year, daily, 9am to 6pm, except Sundays and holidays (11am to 6pm)
Website: www.tourisme-rennes.com - In French only.
Email: infos@tourisme-rennes.com

Street festival. Photo: CRTB

Musée des Beaux-Arts (2)

Quai Émile Zola. An important collection containing works by Veronese, Rubens, Chardin, Corot and Gauguin.
Open: Tue to Sat, 10am to noon, 2pm to 6pm, but closed on Mondays and bank holidays.
Cost: Adult - 4.50€. Free to under 18s and students.

Jardin de Thabor (3)

This 10 hectare (25 acre) park is one of France's most beautiful public gardens. In the 18th century, the site was occupied by an abbey.

Unfortunately the brothers had noisy neighbours, who not only trespassed to chase rabbits, but fired arrows, pistols and carbines, stole the fruit and beat up any monk who dared to intervene. The area was also a popular meeting place for duellists. Perhaps in despair, the Benedictine monks threw open the garden to the public (men only). Thankfully it's a bit more peaceful now (and open to women and children too!) It has a fine collection of trees and three main gardens.

The French Garden
This follows the rules of classical French garden design, with symmetrical borders and square lawns, deep flower beds and paths interspaced with statues. Ponds and fountains enhance the whole.

The Catherinettes Garden
Situated on the site of the hospice of the Catherinettes, who, at the end of the nineteenth century, sheltered ill and needy women. With a rockery, a grotto and waterfall. Terraced, with small paths and a monumental stair marking the entrance from the rue de Paris.

The Roseraie
Roses from the sixteenth to the twenty-first centuries. Roses for beauty, roses for scent and climbing roses.

> **Open:** 7.30am until dusk, all the year round. **Cost:** free.

Parlement de Bretagne (4)
This building once housed the Parliament of Brittany (the English word parliament comes from the French parler, to talk), which was one of the 13 provincial capitals under the Ancien Régime (pre-revolution). It was set up in 1552, twenty years after the annexation of Brittany by the French. The current building dates from the seventeenth century. The parliament now houses a court of appeal.

> **Open:** most days, but only on a guided tour (in French), which must be reserved via the tourist office beforehand.

There are fine half timbered houses to be seen in streets around the **Place Rallier du Baty** and the adjoining **Place and Rue Saint-Michel.**

Place des Lices (5)
Not as unhealthy as it sounds! 'Lice' means jousting in French, and this was once the jousting arena. With some fine buildings. Numbers 26 and 28 are 17th century hotels (mansions) with keel shaped roofs. Nearby are a network of narrow, winding streets, worthy of exploration.

Photo: D. Guillaudeau CRTB

Les Portes Mordelaises (6)

These fifteenth century gates are all that remains of the walls through which the Dukes of Brittany (see 'History of Brittany'), would pass before being crowned. In 1598 the keys were handed over to the French.

Cathedral Saint-Pierre (7)

Dating from 1844 and the third on the site (the first was in the 6th century), this has a very rich interior and a carved Flemish altar piece of the sixteenth century.

Musée de Bretagne

Also worth a visit, this is in the new development of **Les Champs Libres**, just north-east of the railway station. Ask at the tourist office for directions. Breton history, from Neolithic to modern times including a museum of domestic life.

Open: Daily, except Monday and bank holidays, 10am to noon, 2pm to 6pm.
Cost: No information available at time of printing but probably the same as the Musée des Beaux Arts.
Website: www.musee-bretagne.fr - In English too.
Email: museebzh@agglo-rennesmetropole.fr

A Little History

In its two thousand years of history, Rennes began as the capital of the Celtic tribe of the Redonnes, and is now the regional capital for Brittany. It was once the seat of the Dukes of Brittany (see 'History of Brittany').

In 1675 Rennes, followed by the whole of Brittany, rose against taxes on stamps and tobacco. The army was called in and the revolt brutally repressed. The city was largely destroyed by a fire that burned for 6 days in 1720. Much of the present city centre was remodelled and rebuilt at that time.

The first sparks of the French Revolution can be said to have been struck at Rennes (the tinder had been amply prepared by many events, among them the American Revolution), when, in 1789 law students and apprentices demonstrated against the suppression of the Etats de Bretagne (an assembly composed of nobles, clergy and 'the rest') by the King.

Rennes today is a busy and growing town which is heavily involved in cultural activities. It has a metro line.

2.2 Aviary and Gardens

The **Parc ornithologique de Bretagne in Bruz** (35170) is a collection of exotic birds living in botanical and flower gardens. Home to a great variety of budgerigars and parrots, multicoloured pheasants, ducks, geese, swans, birds of prey, touracos, emus and ibis. With a terrace, bar, and picnic area.

Open: July to August, daily, 10am to noon, 2 to 7pm. 1st April to 30th Sept, daily 2pm to 7pm. Feb to April & October, Sundays, 2pm to 6pm.
Cost: Adult - 6.20€. Child (3 to 12) - 3.80€.
Website: www.parc-ornithologique.com

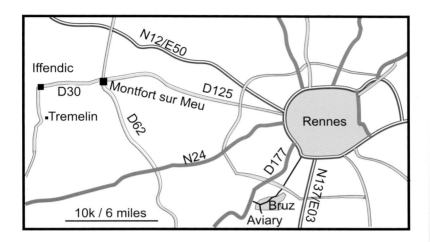

2.3 **Boating and Walking**

The **Domaine de Trémelin in Iffendic** (35750) is a camping area and gite village with leisure activities. It is set in a natural, wooded site covering 220 hectares (about a square mile) around a lake, with water sports, pedal-boats, boats, play areas, quad bikes, forest adventure park, mini-golf, a 5.2 km walk around the lake (about 3.5 miles), bar, supervised lake side beach and a restaurant.

  Cost: Entry is free to the site, priced by attraction.
  Website: www.tremelin.com - with an English page

3. Vitré and Area

An Inspirational Day Out

3.1 Vitré Town - A Medieval Treasure

Population 15,000. Market days are Monday and Saturday, 9am to noon, both days.

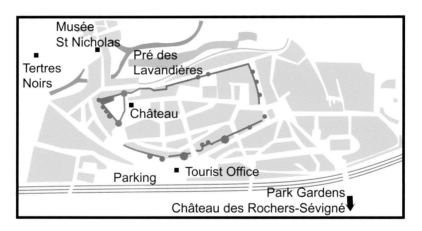

Vitré is located to the east of Rennes, on the very border of Brittany. It is worth the journey to see this wonderful medieval town, the finest example of its kind in Brittany. The beauty of the old town is said to have inspired Victor Hugo and Balzac.

To best appreciate the town, drive up to the **Tertres Noirs Park**. If approaching Vitré from Rennes (on the D857), turn into the Chemin des Tertres Noirs at the roundabout just before the river. The park affords a magnificent view of the castle, the churches and the town's fortifications.

3.2   A Walk around the Town

A good place to start is the **Tourist Office**, Place Général de Gaulle, 35500. They have good brochures, in English and French, and a town map.

Open: July and August, daily 10am to 12.30pm, 2pm to 7pm (Rest of year, closed Monday mornings).
Website: www.ot-vitre.fr (An excellent website, with a version in English).
Email: info@ot-vitre.fr

Photo E.Spiegelhalter, CRTB

Four attractions on 1 ticket. There are 4 attractions to visit in and around Vitré, the castle and 3 museums, as described below. Entry to all of them is by the same ticket, available from any one and valid at all. All of them have the same opening hours:

Open: 1st April to 30th June, daily, 10am to 12.30pm, 2pm to 5.30pm 1st July to 30th September, daily, 10am to 6pm. Rest of year, 10am to noon, 2pm to 5.30pm, but closed Saturday and Sunday mornings.
Cost: (Joint ticket) Adult - 4€. Child (7years -15 years) - 2.50€. Excellent value.

The stunning **castle** dates from the 11th century, and was extensively rebuilt in the four centuries which followed. It has a good museum, which covers the castle's history and also has exhibits on the architecture and decoration of the town's houses. The castle's chapel is fascinating, too, containing 32 splendid Limoges enamels. **The town** itself is well worth exploring. There are many half-timbered houses which date from the 15th and 16th century, their upper storeys jutting out over the street. To enhance the medieval magic, most of the town's **ramparts** are complete.

More prosaically, there are some fine creperies and restaurants here. As well as seeing the town, try and take in a visit to one or more of the museums and gardens mentioned below - they're all worth a look.

The **Pré des Lavandières** – Washerwomen's meadow - is on the banks of the river Vilaine to the north of the castle, the meadow can be reached by a little alley leading off the **Promenade du Val**. This secret garden has aquatic and exotic plants, while flowerbeds add colour. The wash-houses and a former tannery still exist.

The **Musée Saint-Nicholas** is situated in the chapel of the Hospitals of Saint-Yves and Saint-Nicholas, this museum exhibits religious artefacts from the last 150 years. Changes in fashions for religious statuary can be traced through the impressive collection, with some interesting Art Nouveau and Deco pieces. Opening hours as above.

The **Park Gardens** are in the south east part of town 'on the other side of the tracks' (the main Paris to Brest railway line runs through the town), on the D88 (Argentré du Plessis) road, the park has over 50 different species of trees. Cypress, pine, sequoia, cedar, juniper and many more thrive in the English-style park which covers 7ha (17 acres). The park has a deer enclosure. There is a play area. Still follow the D88 (for 6km south of the town) to the…

3.3 Musée des Rochers-Sévigné

An impressive museum in the house where Madame de Sévigné lived when she was in Brittany, and from which she wrote most of her famous letters to her daughter.

Rochers Sevigne - Photo CRTB

Between 1671 and 1696, Madame de Sévigné wrote more than 1,500 letters. She wrote with a very lively style, her letters a mixture of court gossip, confidences, advice, fears, jokes and literary criticism. The Orangery houses a permanent exhibition on the lady and her work, as well as information about the noble family she married into. The chapel is also open to visitors. The grounds are extensive and beautifully laid out, and include a golf course. Opening times and admission charge as above.

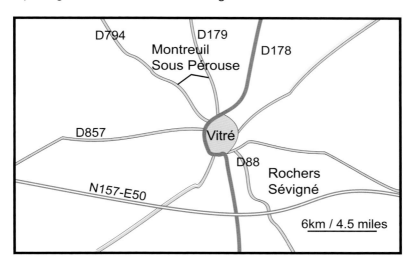

To the north of the town (5km away), at **Montreuil sous Pérouse** is the…

3.4 Musée de la Faucillonnaie

The museum of rural history of the Breton marches. A 15th Century manor house laid out to show rural modes of living over the past six centuries. The farm section of the living museum is particularly interesting, especially for children, as demonstrations are run showing methods of farming from different periods of history. Opening times and admission charge as above.

4. Nantes

Jewel Of The Loire

Nantes: Photo, V. Sarazin, OTNA

Nantes is the sixth largest city in France with half a million inhabitants in the metropolitan area. It was judged by Time magazine in 2003 to be the most pleasant town in France.

There are lots of things to do here, canoeing on the river, rich and rewarding city walks (there are 4 square miles of green spaces in the city), hundreds of kilometres of cycle routes, many museums and galleries and great shopping. It has a vibrant artistic and musical life and is home to many festivals (including the second biggest carnival in France, which takes place in April).

4.1 A Walk around the Town

A good place to start is one of the **Tourist offices**…
3 Cours Olivier de Clisson, 44000. **Open:** Mon to Sat, 10am to 6pm.
2 Place St Pierre (near the Cathedral). **Open:** Tue to Sun, 10am to 1pm,
2pm to 6pm.

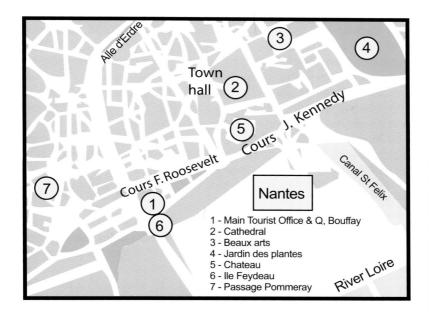

The offices provide a superb range of free maps and guides in English. The **Nantes pass** can also be bought there. This allows entry to all of the attractions here and many others (there are a dozen museums in Nantes). It costs 14€ for 24 hours, under 12's are free. It also allows free use of the public transport system (including the river boats and trams) and 2 hours free bike hire.
   Website: www.nantes-tourisme.com. An excellent site, with an English version.

The **Quartier Bouffay** stands on the original centre of the medieval city (the area to the south of it having largely since been reclaimed from the river Loire). Especially worth seeing here is the **Maison des Apothicaires** (house of the apothecaries), a medieval corner building of jettied construction. The surrounding streets contain some remarkable timber-framed houses, including 7 rue Sainte Croix, 7 rue de la Juiverie and several in rue de la Baclerie. This is the 'Soho' of Nantes, with sunny terraces and exotic restaurants.

The **Cathedrale St-Pierre**, which was begun in 1434, has been destroyed by war and fire and rebuilt several times. Despite this, this flamboyant Gothic cathedral retains a remarkable architectural integrity. See here the astonishing tomb of the parents of Anne of Brittany (her father was Francois the second), which rarely fails to impress the visitor. Look for the enigmatic staue with two faces, one an old man's, the other of a young girl.

The **Musée des Beaux Arts** is one of France's greatest galleries. A rich collection of paintings from the 13th century to the present day. With works by Corbet, Ingres, Chagall and Picasso. Café.

> **Open:** daily, except Thursday, 10am to 6pm
> **Cost:** Free with Nantes Pass, else: Adult - 3.10€. Age 18 to 26 - 1.60€. Under 18 - Free.

Castle - Photo: A. Delaporte, OTNA

The **Jardin des Plantes** is large, with seven hectares (17 acres) of plants. It has many varieties of camellias and greenhouses full of cacti.

There is a children's playground.

The greenhouses are open at 3pm (admission charge, or use the pass).

Castle of the Dukes of Brittany – to re-open in 2007. The chateau dates from the 12th century. It was modified in the 15th century for Francois II, Anne of Brittany's father.

Originally a fortress and ducal palace, the chateau has seen many changes, from royal home to barracks and arsenal, before being transformed into a museum. Important collections of costumes, furniture and on the history of the river and town.

The **Ile Feydeau** is where the rich traders and seamen built their mansions. These have noble facades trimmed with ironwork and ornamented with figureheads. As the name suggests, this was an island in the past, although the branches of the rivers which once surrounded it have now been filled in.

In a city as important as Nantes, one would expect excellent shopping facilities – an expectation that is not disappointed. The **Passage Pommeraye** was opened in 1843. This narrow passage is an architectural wonder. Covered with a glass ceiling, it consists of three levels of shopping galleries dressed up to the nines with stucco arcades, medallions, busts, statues and iron filigree. Most striking is the soft light that bathes this urban oasis. The passage is closed at night.

A Little History

Nantes was originally founded by the Celts. They say that Julius Caesar was the first to place an order for ships here. The city became the capital of the Dukedom of Brittany after the Breton chief Alain Barbe Torte chased out the Normans in 937. This episode marked the beginning of the rivalry between the cities of Nantes and Rennes. It was a great blow for Nantes when, in 1561, parliament was set up in Rennes. The **Edict of Nantes**, which granted freedom from prosecution for Protestants in France, was issued here in 1598. It's revocation had a huge affect on French and English history (see 'History of Brittany') Nantes today is a fast growing and highly regarded city.

5. La Baule and The White Lands

Of Sand, Salt and Snails

5.1   La Baule

Population 16,500. The central market takes place every morning.

This south coast resort is one of the most popular in Brittany. The local tourist board describes its beach as the best in Europe. While this may be a little over the top, it is superb, sheltered to both east and west, stretching for about 5km (3 miles) around the bay to **le Pouliguen**, and sloping gently into the sea.

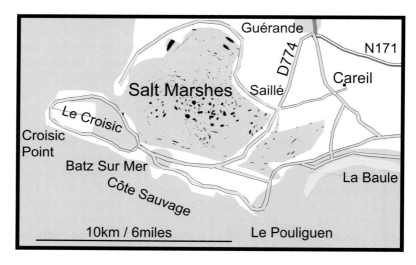

The whole length is lined with luxury hotels, modern buildings and a casino, while the bay is dotted with tiny islands. This elegant seaside resort is much favoured by the French.

The town is a mixture of smart shops, many places to eat and drink, as well as some more downmarket areas with amusement arcades and tacky bars. Overall, however, it is a sophisticated and lively holiday town with something for all the family.

The Tourist Office, at 8 place de la Victoire, 44504, is well worth a visit for its excellent free map of the area and its comprehensive free guide, in English.

Open: July and August, daily, 7.30am to 7.30pm. Rest of year, Monday to Saturday, 9.15am to 12.30pm, 2pm to 6pm, Sunday and bank holidays, 10am to 1pm.
Website: www.labaule.fr (with English version)
Email: tourisme.la.baule@wanadoo.fr

A Little History

On the site of the current town stood the old town of Escoublac, which was buried under shifting sands over a period of centuries. When the railway arrived, in 1879, the new town of La Baule was begun. A massive programme of tree-planting paralleled the building work, to stabilise the sand dunes.

5.2 Along the Coast

Take the road from La Baule across the estuary through **le Pouliguen**, then drive along the (outer) coast, which is called the **Côte Sauvage** (the wild coast), and extends to **le Croisic**.
On the seaward side it alternates between rocks and sandy bays, with many footpaths.
On the landward side are the **White Lands**, the marshes from which salt is extracted. The salt pans, banked enclosures which are flooded by the sea and then gradually dry out under the action of sunlight and wind, are the major feature of this part of the coast.

Before they were constructed, salt was extracted by washing salt-bearing clay and sand. The resulting liquid was then heated in furnaces until the salt crystallised. The demand for wood fuel led to major deforestation locally. The salt pans which replaced this method were constructed from the ninth century until the eighteenth. The salt crystallises in the final basin, from which 3 to 5 kilos of floating crystals ('fine salt') can be raked on a good day, Meanwhile, even greater amounts of salt (up to 50 kilos a day of 'grey salt') forms on the bottom of the pan. There is a viewpoint across the sea just before Batz sur Mer (as well as a world war 2 block house museum).

5.3 Batz Sur Mer – A Town Worth its Salt

Photo - J.P. Gratien, CRTB

Market days are Monday mornings - and also on Friday mornings in July and August. The **Tourist Office** at 25 Rue de la Plage, 44740, has useful maps and leaflets.

Open: July and August, every day, 9.30am to 6.30pm. Rest of year, 9.30am to 12.30pm, 1pm to 5pm, closed Wednesday and Saturday afternoons, and all day Sunday
Email: officetourismebatzsurmer@ wanadoo.fr

Batz has a fine **viewing point**, over the salt pans, from the 57 metre (180ft) tall church belfry.

Open: July and August, daily, 9.30am to 5pm. April, 2pm to 5pm. May and June, 9.30am to noon, 2pm to 5pm. **Cost:** Adult - 1.50€. Child - 0.75€.

There is a **salt museum** at Batz, with amongst its exhibits a reconstructed salt worker's house from the 19th century.
> **Open:** July to September, daily, 10am to 12.30pm, 2pm to 7pm. June and October, Mon to Fri, 10am to noon, Weekends, 2pm to 6pm.
> **Cost:** Adult - 4€. Aged 13 to 18 - €3. Aged 6 to 12 - 2€.

The **salt** from here is very highly regarded. To quote from a retailer: "The unrefined Le Paludier Celtic sea salt is of a light grey colour because of the clay from the salt flats. Some say it is probably the best sea salt on the planet. With nothing added and nothing removed, just the way nature intended The salt is rich in magnesium and other elements." It is widely available locally. There are 2 large and 2 tiny beaches at Batz and numerous places to eat.

At the end of the peninsula, there is a view point at **Pointe du Croisic.**

5.4   Le Croisic and The Aquarium

Le Croisic is a busy port with some interesting old houses in the streets near the church and some fine walks. There are several fine, sandy beaches here, among them **St Goustin** and the smaller **Port Lin**.

Tourist Office (Place de la Gare, 44490).
> **Open:** Daily in July and August. Mon to Sat: 9am to 1pm, 2pm to 7pm. Sun, 10am to 1pm, 3pm to 5pm.
> **Website:** www.ot-lecroisic.com (with English version)
> **Email:** bienvenue@ot-lecroisic.com

There is an **Aquarium** here, with 40 tanks and an enclosed tunnel. It has 200 different species, including Conger eels, Moray eels, sharks, octopuses, tropical turtles, penguins and piranhas. There is a touch pool. The visit takes about 2 hours. There is a leaflet in English.

The aquarium has a shop, café and picnic area. The penguins are fed at 11am, 3pm and 5pm.

Open: June, July and August from 10am to 7pm. Most other months: 10am to noon, 2pm to 6pm.
Cost: Adult -11€. Child (3-12) - 8€.
Website: www.ocearium-croisic.fr (in French only)

If you're feeling intrepid, there's even a snail farm and tasting room nearby. Details from the tourist office!

Photo J.P. Gratien, CRTB

5.5 Saillé

La Maison des Paludiers (salt worker's house). The visit lasts for about an hour. With models of the extraction process and a film, with a version in English.

Open: June, July and August, daily, 10am to 12.30pm, 2pm to 6pm.
Cost: Adult - 4€. Child (6-14) - 2.80€. Under 6 – Free. For a little extra, you can also go on a 1.5 hour guided tour of a working salt extraction.
Email: maisonpaludiers@free.fr

Return bypassing Guérande (dealt with in the section on the Black Lands) to the…

5.6 Chateau de Careil

An interesting chateau sited between La Baule and Guérande, showing Breton architecture between the 14th and 16th centuries. The chateau played an important part in the wars of religion (see history section). The tour is a guided one, in French and English (except the 5pm one, which is in French only).

Open: conducted tours every day from June 1st till August 31st at 11am, 3pm, 4pm, 5pm, 6pm. In July and August, candle-lit visits also take place on Monday and Wednesday at 9.30pm.
Cost: Over 12's and adults - 5€. Age 5 to 12 - 4€. Under 5's - free
Website: www.paysblanc.com/chateau-careil
Email: chateau.careil@free.fr

6. Guérande and the Black Lands

Messing Around in the Marshes

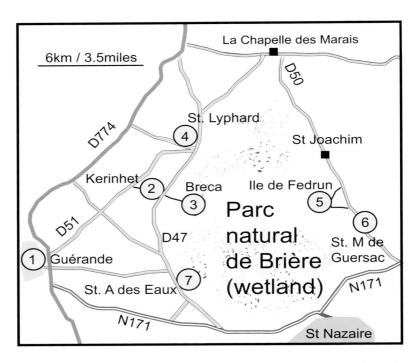

The route described below will take you around the **Grande Brière**, one of the largest wetlands in France, from which peat has traditionally been extracted (hence the name 'black lands'). This is a national park and an important area for migrating birds. There are quite a few places locally where you can get punts into the marsh. I have mentioned two (in Breca and the Ile de Fedrun) where the guides speak English.

6.1 Guérande – A Fine Walled Town

Guérande. Population 13600. Market days are on Wednesday and Saturday mornings.

This town, beloved of the Dukes of Brittany, dominates two landscapes: the White Lands - **le Pays Blanc** - salt marshes which stretch down to the coast (see the day out 'La Baule and the White Lands') and the Black Lands (**le Pays Noir**), of peat. Guérande has been loved by some of the great French writers, such as Flaubert and, above all, Balzac, and is a very popular place with tourists.

The **Tourist Office**, 1 place du Marché au Bois, 44350, give out **excellent free local maps** and a free local guide in three languages. They also do guided tours with several themes (history, fortifications, religious, architecture) in season. These are 1 - 2 hours and cost 5.50€ for an adult, 2.50€ for children aged 6 - 12 (under 6's free). Some are in English.

> **Open:** July and August, daily 9.30am to 7pm, except Sunday, 10am to 1pm, 3pm to 5pm. June and September: 9.30am to 12.30pm, 1.30pm to 6pm, closed Sundays and bank holidays.
> **Website:** www.ot-querande.fr - in French only.
> **Email:** contact@ot-guerande.fr

The medieval city has an almost complete set of ramparts. There is a **museum** in the principal one of the ancient gateways to the town, the Porte Saint- Michel. Local history over 3 floors, including furniture, 30 mannequins in costume, Breton bonnets and an armoury. Included in the entrance fee is access to part of the town ramparts.

> **Open:** April to October, inclusive, daily, 10am to 12.30pm, 2pm to 6pm.
> **Cost:** Adult - 3.50€. Child (6 to 17) - 2€. Under 6 – free.

There is also a **doll and toy museum** in the town (same opening times as the museum).

> Adult - 4€. Child (6 to 10) - 2€. Under 6 – free.

There are over a dozen places to eat in the town.

A Little History

Guérande has been occupied since Neolithic times, as the standing stones in the area attest. The current town is said to have been founded in the sixth century. In the ninth century it was the seat of a bishop, while a castle, built about the year 1000, allowed the town to grow further.

It was sacked by a combined French and Spanish army in 1342, after which, over a period of a century, the town was massively fortified. The later development of the town was due to the trade in salt and wine, for it had an important shipping fleet. However silting put an end to its importance, and it slept away the centuries until its recent 'rediscovery' by writers and tourists.

Guérande - photo CRTB

6.2 Kerhinet - Thatches in the Marshlands

A small pedestrian only village restored to as it would have been in 1875. The reed and bulrush thatched cottages give it a fairy-tale feel. With explanation boards in French and English. There is no charge to look round the village (the houses are privately owned and not open to the public), which has a creperie. There is a small museum here:

Open: April – June, daily, 2pm to 6pm. July – Sept, daily, 10.30am to 1pm, 2.30pm to 6.30pm.
Cost: Adult - 5€. Child 2.50€.

6.3   Bréca - Punting

A hamlet 5 km (3 miles) south of Saint Lyphard on the D47. From the harbour, the company **La Faune Briéronne** hires **punts into the marsh**, and **trips by horse and cart**, with a commentary in English (in season).

Open: Daily - 9am to 7pm
Cost: Punt with Oarsman (45mins) Adult - 7€. Child (4 to 14) - 4€. Under 4 – free. Punt and horse and cart trip (90 mins): Adult - 12€. Child - 6€. Punts can also be hired without a guide/oarsman for a very reasonable charge (1-3 persons, 20€, 4 - 6 persons 25€, no time limit).
Website: http://faunebrieronne.free.fr - in French only.

There are 2 signposted walking routes here too, one is 4km (2.5 miles), the other 7km (4.5 miles). Great for bird watching.

6.4   Saint Lyphard – A View from the Tower

Market day Thursday. There are restaurants and creperies in the village. This commune, sited on the western edge of the second largest marsh in France, has many thatched cottages. There is a fine view of the marshes from the **Belvedere** (bell tower), ascent partly by fixed ladders.

Open: July and August, daily, every half hour from 10am to 6.30pm, but not 12.30pm & 1pm. April, May, June, Sept, Mon to Sat, every half hour from 10.30am to 5.30pm, but not 12.30pm, 1pm and 1.30pm.
Cost: Adult - 3€. Child (5 to 12) - 1.50€. This visit is not suitable for under 5's. Tickets from (and guide supplied by) the Tourist Office, opposite.

The area has known violent times. The vicar of St Lyphard in 1789, Julien Landeau, hid himself so as not to have to swear loyalty to the revolutionary government.

He was discovered and taken to Nantes, where he was imprisoned, until the sinister Carrier had him taken with many other priests on a boat which was sunk in the middle of the Loire (Carrier drowned 3,000 people in this way). Landeau was rescued and hidden by fishermen. When he finally died he was buried under a false name.

The **Tourist Office**, Place de l'Église, 44410, have a useful local guide in English and French, telling about the history and wildlife of the wetlands.

> **Open:** July and August, 10am to noon, 1.30pm to 7pm. April, May, June, Sept, Mon to Sat, 10.30am to 12.30pm, 1.30pm to 6pm.
> **Website:** www.saint-lyphard.com - In French only
> **Email:** St-lyphard@tiscali.fr

Photo - J.P, Gratien, CRTB

6.5 Ile de Fedrun

A punt trip (with oarsman) of around an hour around this interesting island in the marshes. Some guides speak English.

> **Open:** Every day in summer, 8am to 8pm.
> **Cost:** Adult - 7€. Child (3 to 12) - 4€.

6.6 Maison de l'Eclusier/ Pierre Constant Reserve

(Lock keeper's house). **Saint Malo De Guersac**. A museum covering turf extraction, punt construction and the history, geology and life of the marshes. From here, a 10 minute walk can be taken to the **Pierre Constant bird reserve**, where there are walks of about a mile, many hides and a fantastic variety of birds and wildlife (including Ibis, Coypu and otters). English spoken.

> **Open:** July to end Sep, 10.30am to 1pm, 2.30pm to 6.30pm. April to June, 2pm to 6pm. Cost: (joint ticket) Adult - 5€. Child - 2.50€.
> **Website:** www.parc-naturel-briere.com - In French only.

6.7 Ker Anas Wildfowl Sanctuary

Saint André des Eaux
This is a 4 hectare (10 acre) park. All the birds in the Ker Anas sanctuary are of the duck family. There are 247 different species in the world – of which there are more than a hundred to be seen here. With lakes, picnic tables and about a kilometre of track. There is a gift shop and a terrace bar. English spoken. Approximate visit time is 1.5 to 2 hours.

> **Open:** July and August, daily, 10am to 8pm. April to June and September, daily, 2.30pm to 6.30pm.
> **Cost:** Adult - 5.80€. School children - 3.20€. (bird food 0.50€). Under 5 - free. **Website:** www.keranas.fr - In French only.

7. Vannes and The Gulf

Of Coast, Castle and Kids

As always with our days out, we give you a choice of several attractions, so that you can pick and mix depending on your circumstances. Today is perhaps the fullest day of all, for not only is there a splendid city, a magnificent coastal drive and a magical castle, there is also a great children's attraction…

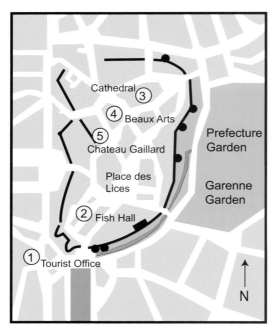

7.1 **Vannes**
Population 55,000

Vannes is the capital of the Morbihan department of Brittany. Morbihan owes its name to the gulf, or inner sea (Mor Bihan being Breton for little sea) on which Vannes lies. Vannes retains much of its town wall, including seven gates. Within these ramparts, around the cathedral, are nearly 200 buildings, many of them half-timbered, of the 16th and 17th centuries. The best shopping is to be found there.

A Short Walk Around the Town

A good place to start is the **Tourist Office** - 1 Rue Thiers, 56000. They provide a leaflet, in English, for a very interesting town walk, giving more detail of the town's attractions than I have space to do here. They also give out an excellent general map of the area. As there is very often a festival in Vannes, of music, sailing, or street theatre, it is worth enquiring about what is currently going on. If you are considering a boat trip in the gulf, this is the place to ask for details.

Open: July and August, daily 9am to 7pm except Sundays and bank holidays, 10am to 6pm. Out of season, Monday to Saturday, 9.30am to 12.30pm, 2pm to 6pm.
Website: www.tourisme-vannes.com - in French only.
Email: info@tourisme-vannes.com

The Fish Hall - Monday to Saturday 7am to 1pm. Very busy, especially so on market days – Wednesdays and Saturdays.

The Ramparts (when you can find them!) - Built during the 13th century from which there are fantastic views. Look out for the lavoirs (wash houses) in the gardens below.

Cathedral of St. Peter (13th - 19th cent.) - Contains the tomb (and skull, in a glass case) of St. Vincent Ferrer (an evangelist who died here in 1419). Some fine statues, copes and mitres.

Musée des Beaux Arts (la Cohue) - Place st Pierre. The gallery shows pieces by Monet and Delacroix, as well as works by Breton artists.

Open: mid June to end September, daily, 10am to 6pm. Rest of year, 10am to noon, 2pm to 6pm, closed on Tuesday, and on Sunday morning.
Cost: Age 12 and over - 4€. Under 12 – free. A joint ticket can be purchased for the Chateau Gaillard for 6€.

Château Gaillard: An outstanding display of prehistoric (Neolithic) items, as well as some more modern displays, sited in the former House of Parliament of Brittany.

Open: Mid June to end September, daily 10am to 6pm. Rest of year: only during school holidays, in the afternoons.
Cost: Age12 and over - 3.50€. Under 12 – free. A joint ticket can be purchased for the Musée des Beaux Arts for 6€.

A Little History

Vannes is the one-time Roman Darioritum, the capital of the Vénètes (they also had relatives in Italy who founded Venice). For the fate of the Vénètes, read about the Mound of Tumiac, below. The emperor Probus had the town walled in the 3rd century and it was the meeting point of several Roman roads. In the time of the Breton

kings, Waroc'h had the ramparts rebuilt. In the Middle Ages continual battles were fought between the Franks and Bretons for possession of the town. In 919, Vannes was pillaged and burned by the Vikings, their first, and typical, taste of the people who would become their Norman neighbours. In 1154 the Arab geographer Idrisi described the town as 'one of the principal cities of Brittany.. at the end of the gulf, a pleasant and populous spot, where there is a port and shipyard.' The

Vannes - photo: J.P. Gratien, CRTB

Parliament of Brittany sat at Vannes from 1514 for 14 years and would sit there again, after the union of Brittany with France. In the 17th century Vannes indulged in slave trading and piracy. Now it calls itself 'the most dynamic small town in France'. With its plethora of festivals and events, it's difficult to argue with the description.

7.2   The Aquarium, Butterfly Park & Port

An impressive **Aquarium**, (to the south west of the town, next to the gare maritime), is home to 600 species of fish, sharks, sea turtles and species native to the area, such as cuttlefish and sea horses. It has a bar and crêperie from 1st May to September - and a gift shop.

Open: July and August, daily, from 9am to 7.30pm. April to June and Sept to Oct, daily, 10am to 12.30pm, 2pm to 6.30pm. **Cost:** Age 12 and over - 8.90€. Age 4 to 11 years – 5.90€. Under 4 - Free. Joint ticket with the butterfly park: Adult - 13€ Child - 9€. **Website:** www.aquarium-du-golfe.com (with English version).

There is a splendid **Butterfly Park**, with 10,000 butterflies in a tropical glass house and many orchids (situated next to the aquarium). No shop or restaurant.

Open: July and August, daily, from 10am to 7.30pm. April to June and Sept to Oct, daily, 10am to 12.30pm, 2pm to 6.30pm. **Cost:** Age 12 and over – 7.50€. Age 4 to 11 years - 5.50€. Under 4 - free. For price for a joint ticket with the aquarium, see above. **Website:** www.jardinauxpappilons.com (with English version).

In the bay there are a number of ships providing passage to the many islands in the Gulf of Morbihan. Details available from the tourist office or at the gare maritime.

7.3 The Séné Nature Reserve

At Séné, follow the signs for the **Réserve naturelle**. The gulf of Morbihan is an important place for migrating birds.

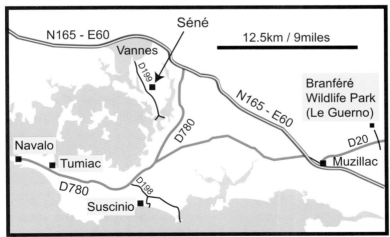

Tens of thousands pass through each year. This nature reserve was created in 1996 to protect about 400 acres of salt marsh and salt pans. 200 species of birds can be seen here. Here also can be seen the basins used for taking salt from the marshes.

Open: July and August, daily 10am to 1pm, 2pm to 7pm. 1st Feb to 30th June, Sundays and bank holidays, 10am to 1pm, 2pm to 7pm.

Cost: Adult - 4€. Students and school children - 2.50€. Under 12 - Free.

7.4   The Tumulus of Tumiac (Butte de César)

Is a 10 minute walk from the D780 (signposted). From the tumuli there are superb views of the bay, the gulf and the islands. From here Julius Caesar is supposed to have watched the naval battle in 56 BC between the Romans and the Venetii. Decimus Brutus, the young future assassin of Caesar, was sent to build a fleet against the Venetii, a rich tribe local to this area who owed part of their wealth from shipping tin from Britain. This move, while partly designed to establish authority over the whole of Gaul, was also a precursor to the invasion of Britain. The Venetii controlled the waterways with a formidable fleet of their own and were augmented by British Celts. At first the Gallic vessels outmatched the Romans, and Brutus could do little to hamper Venetii operations. Roman ingenuity took over, however, and they began using hooks launched by archers to grapple the Venetii ships to their own. Before long, the Venetii were completely defeated, and like many tribes before them, those who were not slaughtered on the spot were sold into slavery. As ever with the Romans, they, as the historian Tacitus recorded, 'created a desert and called it peace.' With the defeat of the Gallic resistance, Caesar launched two attacks on Britain. These were not successful, and Caesar returned to Rome to attend to political matters - and one last meeting with Brutus...

7.5   Port Navalo / Arzon / Port de Crouesty

Port Navalo, an ancient fishing village, is now joined to Arzon and Port de Crouesty. Here are luxurious residences, hotels, supermarkets, a casino and one of the largest marinas in France.

The harbour of Port de Crouesty is busy, with tourist and sailing boats, bars and restaurants. There is a very good beach to the south. At the western point (Port Navalo) is a light house and two more nice sandy beaches. Everywhere there are great coastal walks and views of the 'big sea' and the 'little sea' and across to Locmariaquer, on the other side of the narrow strait.

The **Tourist Office**, Rond-point du Crouesty, 56640, supplies useful local maps, including cycle routes.

> **Open:** July and August, Monday to Saturday, 9am to 12.30pm, 2pm to 7pm. Sunday, 10am to 1pm. Rest of year, Mon to Sat, 9am to noon, 2pm to 6pm.
> **Website:** www.crouesty.fr
> **Email:** crouesty@crouesty.fr

7.6 Suscinio Castle

An impressive 14th-century moated castle set in marshland at the edge of a tiny village, on the southern edge of the Gulf of Morbihan, once the summer residence of the Dukes of Brittany.

Suscinio Castle: Photo: CRTB

The Dukes moved about a great deal, but Suscinio was one of their favourite residences. Their entourages were huge. In 1305, when Duke Jean II went to Lyon to assist at the crowning of the Pope, he was accompanied by 90 people (the Duke was to die on this trip). The castle passed to the French crown in 1520 and over the following centuries fell more and more into ruin until it was used as a stone quarry. Thankfully it has been massively restored in the last 40 years and is now a museum.

Open: From April to September, daily between 10am and 7pm (for the rest of the year, it closes on Wednesdays and between noon and 2pm).

Cost: Adult - 6€. Child (8 to 17) - 2€. Under 8 - free. There is a gift shop, and a creperie 200 yards away.

Website: www.suscinio.info - In French only

Email: suscinio@sagemor.fr

7.7   Wildlife & Botanic Park

Parc Animalier et Botanique de Branféré in Le Guerno – 56190. A botanical safari park with 150 species of animals from around the world, including lemurs, wallabies, tapirs, zebras and many more: 2000 creatures in all. You can feed the animals at the "Meet the animals" corner. A haven for an interesting mix of easy going wildlife, which coexists harmoniously in delightful surroundings. As well as the animals, there are a fine selection of trees and plants. With a panoramic restaurant, a terrace bar, picnic areas outside the park and a gift shop.

Open: (The park closes an hour and a half after these times): May, June, July, August, daily, 10am to 6pm. April & September, daily, 10am to 5pm. Feb, March, October and November: daily, 2pm to 4.30pm.

Cost: Adult - 11€. Child (4 to 12 inclusive) – 8€.

Website: www.branfere.com - In French only

Email: contact@branfere.com

8. Josselin and Paimpont

Of Knights, Forest and Enchantment

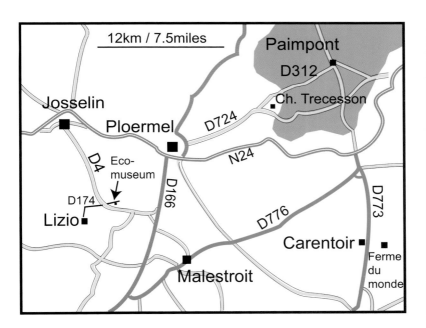

8.1   Josselin and its Castle

Market, Saturday morning. An attractive and historic small town on the Nantes to Brest canal.

The **Tourist Office**, Place de la Congregation, 56120, furnishes useful maps of the surrounding area.

> **Open:** July and August, daily (including bank holidays), 10am to 6pm.
> April to June & September, Mon to Sat, 10am to noon, 2pm to 6pm. Other months,
> Mon to Fri, 9.30am to noon, 2pm to 5.30pm. Sat 9.30 to noon
> **Website:** www.paysdejosselin-tourisme.com – In French only.
> **Email:** ot.josselin@wanadoo.fr

The chief attraction of the town is its very fine **Castle**. It is one of the few Breton castles which is still the property of one of the old ruling families, in this case the Rohans. It was built in the 6th century, destroyed by the 14th century and rebuilt by Olivier de Clisson. It came into the ownership of the Rohan family in the 16th century. The internal façade is quite different from the military one seen from the river. The tour of the chateau takes you round five extravagantly decorated rooms, the rest still being lived in by the family. Look out for the letter 'A' woven into the designs, for the much loved Anne of Brittany.

Josselin castle - Photo: A. Bobrovitch, CRTB

There is a **Dolls' Museum** on the same site, housing 600 dolls, houses and accessories. Begun in 1880 and growing ever since, it has dolls from the 17th to the 20th centuries.

Open: July and August, daily, 10am to 6pm. June & Sept, daily, 2pm to 6pm. April May, Oct, Sat, Sun, and school holidays, 2pm to 6pm.
Cost: Chateau (45 minute guided visit, in French) Adult - 7€. Child (7 to 14) - 4.80€. Dolls' house: Adult - 6.20€. Child - 4.40€. Combined ticket: (Chateau & Dolls' Museum) Adult - 12€. Child - 8.40€.

From the castle, in 1351, after being blessed by the church, thirty Breton knights rode out to meet thirty English and allied knights for a battle. They met mid-way between Josselin and Ploermel. The affray took part in the Breton civil war, which was part of the Hundred Year War between England and France (see the history section).

The arranged combat was led by Robert de Beaumanoir from Josselin and Robert Bemborough, the English champion from the Ploermel garrison. The knights used daggers and axes. When a break was called, two English and four Bretons were already dead. Beaumanoir is said to have called for a drink, to which Bemborough charmingly replied: 'drink your own blood'. The battle, after it was resumed, ended with French victory, when eight of Bemborough's men were dead and the rest taken for ransom. It is worth having a wander round the town, with its narrow streets and timber framed houses. The River Oust (doubling as the Nantes Brest canal) runs through the town: and river cruises are run from here. There are plenty of restaurants and shops.

8.2 Ploermel
Market Day Friday

A charming small town, once the seat of the Dukes of Brittany, with some interesting buildings. All services. It is worth starting at the **Tourist Office**, 5 rue du Val, 56804. The office supplies brochures of the area, including a first class series of cycling and walking routes (free), four of them in English, giving an excellent choice of local walks – around the town and country - varying in length from 2.8 to 11 kilometres (about 2 to 7 miles).
Open: July and August, Mon to Sat, 9.30am to 7pm, Sun and bank hols, 10am to 12.30pm. Rest of year, Mon to Sat, 10am to 12.30pm, 2pm to 6.30pm

8.3 Paimpont - Merlin's Forest

Paimpont, a pretty village with some services (two creperies, grocer, baker and butcher), is a good starting point for exploring the forest of the same name. There is a lovely abbey next to a small lake here. The **Tourist Office**, 5, Esplanade de Brocéliande, 35380, is worth visiting for the small free map 'the legendary sites of the forest of Paimpont' (in French). This is a useful map to find a number of, directionally rather tricky, sites in the forest.

Open: June to Sep, daily 10am to noon, 2pm to 6pm. Oct to March (not Jan), daily, except Monday, 10am to noon, 2pm to 5pm

Website: www.paimpont.fr - In French only

Email: syndicat-dinitiativepaimpont@wanadoo.fr

Photo: A Bobrovitch, CRTB

8.4 Paimpont Forest

What was once part of the super-forest of Broceliande, is the cradle of the Arthurian legend in Brittany, and it was here that Merlin and the fairy Viviane were supposed to have lived. A drive through the forest will be enough to give you a sense of why so many legends surround these dense and silent woods, but if the weather is good and you're a confident walker (preferably with a compass), it's best to get off the road and into the body of the forest, which once covered the whole of Brittany. The sorceress Morgan's **Val sans retour** (valley of no return) should be high on your list of places to visit in the forest.

Legend has it that the jilted Morgan la Fay put a spell on the valley so that unfaithful knights could never leave. Fortunately Lancelot lifted the curse, so no one should be afraid to visit today. The **Tombeau de Merlin** – Merlin's tomb, is where the fairy Viviane trapped Merlin by making nine magic circles around him. There are many signposted walks – but remember that it is easy to get lost in a forest.

Look out for the **Chateau de Trecesson** as it is very beautiful but not open to the public: which is just as well, as it is said to be haunted.

8.5 Ferme Du Monde – Wildlife Park

At **Carentoir**. A wooded park of 400 livestock animals from all continents living in the semi-wild: yaks, camels, buffalos, and wild pigs. There are 5 zones, each representing a continent. At the children's farm you can stroke the animals or have a pony ride. There is a shop, bar, café and exhibition room.

Open: 1st April until mid November, 9am to 7pm.
Cost: Adult - 8€. Student - 4.50€. Under 6 - free. The site is easy to walk around, although there is also a small train for an extra 2€ each.
Website: www.lafermedumonde.com - In French only

8.6 Malestroit – Walks & Cycling

Market day: Thursday

This picturesque town contains interesting Gothic houses, and is situated on the river Oust. The Nantes Brest canal runs through the town. There are walks and cycle routes from and around the town. The **Tourist Office**, 17 place du Bouffay, 56140, provides a most helpful range of leaflets, including a very useful 32 page guide to the area, 'visits and discoveries de l'Oust a Broceliande' (English version available).

Open: 1st July to 31st Aug, 9am to 7pm (Sun 10am to 4pm). Rest of year, 9.30am to 12.30pm, 2.30pm to 6.30pm.
Website: www.malestroit.com - In French and English.

8.7   Lizio - Farm Museum and More

Lizio is a "petite cité de caractère" (small town of historical interest) with fine and dignified granite residences dating from the 16th century. For such a small place, there's a lot to see. As well as the Ecomuseum (see below), there is also the Poète Ferrailleur (scrap merchant poet) Museum, a fabulous imaginary universe of moving objects, created from scrap. There is a Boar farm (with tastings), an Insectarium, and close by, a Museum of the French resistance. Leaflets for all of these can be had from the tourist office at Malestroit.

The Ecomuseum - 56460, Lizio

A large museum with 70,000 exhibits. A series of Breton interiors with their traditional box-beds, wardrobes and clocks. Add period shops (clock shop, chemists, dress shop, etc), a school room, tradesmen's workshops and you can see there is a lot to see here. Great fun. The museum is a labour of love of its founder Alain Guillard, whom you will probably meet. There is a picnic area, and a shop which sells a fantastic range of clockwork toys.

Open: 1st April – 30th September, 10am to noon, 2pm to 7pm. Oct, Feb, March, 2pm to 6pm. Closed Saturday and Sunday mornings, except in July and August.**Cost:** Adult - 5.50€. Child (5 to 12) - 4€. Under 5 - free.
Website: www.ecomuseelizio.com - In French only.

9. Pontivy and Guerlédan Lake

At the Heart of Brittany

Pontivy. Population 15,000. Market day is all day Monday. Food market, Saturday morning in July, Aug, Sep. Post code – 56300.

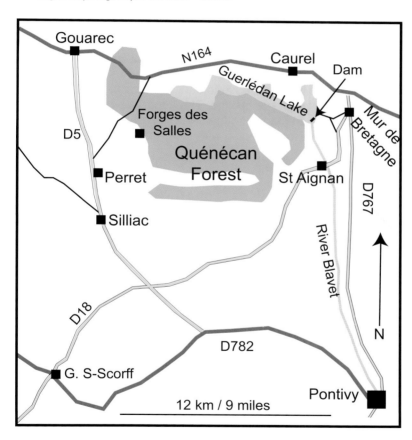

9.1 Pontivy

This medieval town occupies a beautiful position on the river Blavet at the very centre of Brittany. After the revolution, Napoleon decided to make it the strategic centre of Brittany. He built extensively around the existing town, the population renaming it Napoleonville. The name has since reverted to Pontivy. The town is a double treat, having both the grandeur of Napoleon's imperial city and the beauty of the medieval core. Stroll around the **old town**, taking time to admire the half-timbered buildings: particularly around the **Rue du Fil** (thread street), the **Place du Martray** (Martray Square) and the **Rue du Pont**. The Napoleonic quarter is centred around **la Plaine**, the old parade ground. The contrast between its formal design and straight roads and the medieval area is startling. This is an excellent town for shopping with supermarkets on the outskirts.

Photo: C. Archambaud - CRTB

The original castle was destroyed by the English in 1342. The existing castle was completed in 1485, and is regarded as being one of the finest examples of medieval architecture in existence.

Open: July and August, daily, 10.30am to 7.30pm. Rest of the season, Wed to Sun, 10am to noon, 2pm to 6pm.
Cost: Adult – 4.30€. Age 13 to 20 – 2.70€. Under 13 – 1.90€.

A Little History

The town is named after Ivy, a monk who came from Northumberland and founded it in the 7th century. The castle was built by the Rohans at the end of the 15th century. At the time of the revolution, the townspeople were heavily on the side of the republic (in sharp contrast with the surrounding countryside, where the peasants were strongly royalist). Partly in gratitude for their support, Napoleon decided to make the town the military and strategic centre of Brittany. Two other reasons also played a part in the decision. The first was the position of the town, right at the heart of Brittany. The other was that, due to the British Royal Navy, coastal navigation between Brest and Nantes had become dangerous, so the Emperor decided to build a canal linking the two ports. Pontivy was about half-way between them.

9.2   Around the Guerlédan lake

The 12km long Guerlédan lake is the largest in Brittany. It is set in beautiful forested country about 15km (10 miles) north of Pontivy. There is a small **Electrical museum** about a mile south of the lake, at **St Aignan**.
Open: June to September, 9.30am to 12.30pm, 2.30pm to 6.30pm (except Sunday, afternoons only).
Cost: Adult – 3.10€. Under 18 – 1.55€.

The **Barrage at Guerlédan**, which is 46m (155 feet) high, is the largest dam in Brittany. Several circular colour-coded walks of between 10 and 13 kilometres (6 to 8 miles), start at, or near, the dam. A free map of the walks can be had from the Tourist Office in **Mur de Bretagne**.

The tourist office is open all the year round, Monday to Saturday, 10am to 12.30pm and 2pm to 5pm (6 in the summer). Closed Sunday, except in July and August, when open from 10.30am to 2pm. If you're feeling sedentary you can take a 1.5 hour cruise on the lake, from **Caurel**. Daily at 3pm.

Cost: Adult - 8.60€. Child (3-10) - 5.60€. Pedal boats can also be hired here.

Photo: CRTB

9.3   Les Forges des Salles - Iron Works Museum

An unusual but interesting attraction in the heart of the forest, near Perret, is the ironworking village dating from the 18th century. At the village, of about 30 buildings, can be seen not only the different processes in iron working, but also village and communal life (school, chapel, canteen). Water being essential in making iron, there are three lakes around the village.

Open: July and August, daily, 2pm to 6.30pm. April to June, Sept and Oct, weekends only, 2pm to 6.30pm.

Cost: Adult - 5€. Child (10-17) - 3€. Under 10 - free.

10. Auray, Gavrinis and the Monks Isle

Of Battles, Builders and Monks

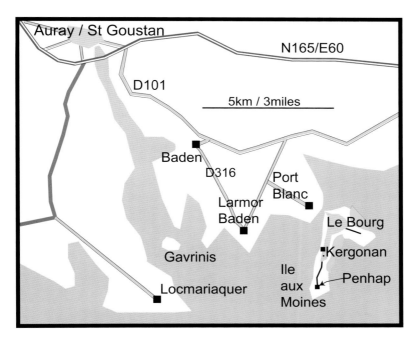

10.1 Auray - Town of Many Battles

Auray. Population 10000. Market, Monday morning. Fruit & Veg market, Friday morning. Post code 56400.

Auray is a situated on the river Loch. To the east of the river is the port of **St Goustan**, the oldest and most picturesque part of the town. Once it was a major fishing port but now it is more peaceful and an inspiration for numerous painters, with its 15th century half-timbered houses which give onto the quay. There are a number of fine restaurants in the town, especially fish ones.

There is a **Tourist office** who supply a map of the town with a suggested walking route around it. Opening times not available at time of printing.

> **Website:** www.auray-tourisme.com
> **Email:** contact@ville-auray.fr

A Little History

Auray is the prime contender to have been the site of the naval battle where Caesar's navy overcame the Venetii resistance, then slaughtered that part of the population which had no value to them and sold the rest into slavery (see Vannes day out). History is often a record of battles, alas, and Breton history more so than most. The War of Succession (1312 – 1364) ended with the Battle of Auray and the death of one of the warring cousins on the battle field.

St Goustan. Photo: J.Piriou, CRTB

In 1776, Benjamin Franklin, man of science, politician and philosopher, was designated by Congress to seek France's help in the War of Independence that America was fighting against Britain. A small warship, the Reprisal, was to bring him to Nantes, but adverse winds forced him to anchor in the bay at Quiberon. Franklin went up the Auray River in a rowboat and landed at St. Goustan, from where he travelled to Nantes by postchaise. There is a Benjamin Franklin school at Auray. The example of the successful American revolt was to be a major factor in the French Revolution, which took place just 13 years later. A British link is with the Choauns (French royalists who fought against the revolution). Britain, as a monarchy, supported European monarchy and intervened to try and restore the monarchy to France (as she was also to try to do in Russia after the overthrow of the Czar). These attempts, which included the landings at Quiberon (see the entry on Quiberon), ended when the French nobility who took part in that landing were shot at Auray.

10.2   The Tumulus on Gavrinis Island

The tiny island of **Gavrinis** measures 750 yards by 450 and is home to one of the finest megalithic monuments in the world (for much more about megalith standing stones, see the section on Carnac). This monument 8m (25ft) wide and 8m (25ft) high, has a corridor 13m (40ft) long leading to a burial chamber. The chamber itself is made of 40 pieces of stone, some of them weighing 17 tons. All of the slabs of stone are carved with spiralling lines. Gavrinis can be visited between April and November, via a fifteen-minute ferry ride from **Larmor-Baden**. Ticket prices include a guided tour. However, **as the number of places are limited, it is strongly advised to reserve in advance**. Your local tourist office may help you with this. The ferry operator's telephone number is 02.97.57.19.38.

Ferry times: July & Aug, daily except Wed, 9.30am to noon, 2pm to 5pm. April, June & Sept, daily, except Wed, 9.30am to 11.00am, 2pm to 4.30pm. May, Mon to Fri, 1.30pm to 4.30pm, Sat & Sun, 9.30am to 11am & 1.30pm to 4.30pm. Oct & Nov, daily, except Wednesday, 1.30pm to 3pm.

Cost: (Admission & Ferry) Adult - 10€. Age 8 to 17 - 9€. Under 8 - free.

10.3 Port Blanc to the Monk's Island

The Ile aux Moines is about 3.5 miles long and 2 wide (at its widest). The island has some delights, but, because it has been allowed to become over developed around the town (Le Bourg), it takes a while to get to them. Balanced against this is that the island is quick to get to and the crossing cheap (hence the over development perhaps). So, if you go there, if you're walking, reckon on an hour to clear the town. There are 3 cycle hire shops (about 10€ per bike per day).

There is a tourist information office at the port (closed between 12.30pm and 2pm) which supplies a useful map of the island. **Le Bourg** has about a dozen places to eat, plus a supermarket, baker (closed Monday), bookshop and gift shops. The island has a large sandy beach and several small ones. The island's warm and mild climate allows palm trees, mimosas, camellias and figs to grow. At **Kergonan** there are 24 menhirs, the remaining part of a large stone circle. At **Pen Hap**, the major dolmen of the island consists of an off-centered corridor and a rectangular chamber.

Getting there

The ferry, from Port Blanc, leaves half hourly every day of the year, the crossing taking 5 minutes.

> **Cost:** (return) Age 11 and over - 4€. Age 4 to 10 - 2€. Under 4 – free. (Bikes 3€). **Website:** www.izenah-croisieres.com - with a good English version.

11. Erdeven and Carnac

Stones of Awe

Brittany is famous for its prehistoric menhirs (single upright stones) and dolmens (stone tables or barrows, that is with two or more uprights and a cap stone). They are immensely old (pre-dating the Egyptian pyramids), they occur everywhere in the countryside and they generally have a link with water, single menhirs being often sited where two streams join underground. If Brittany is the worldwide centre of these astonishing monuments, then here, just south of Auray, is the bullseye.

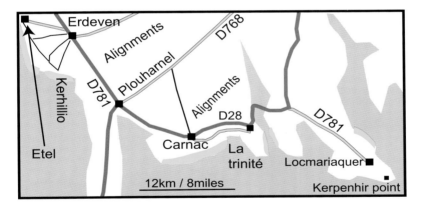

11.1 Erdeven

Population 2600. Market day, Thursday (there is also an evening market in July and August, on Mondays, between 6pm and 10pm).

Erdeven is a good place to visit ancient stones and yet avoid the crowds at Carnac (where the stones are fenced off anyway). Erdeven has several eating places, local shops, a supermarket and the tourist office.

The **Tourist Office**, 7, Rue Abbé-Le-Barh (in the centre). 56410, gives out a very good **free motoring map of the area** (courtesy of La Belle-Iloise, the cannery mentioned in the section on Quiberon) and a guide pamphlet of local attractions (English sections), which includes a **town map showing the megalith trail**. Also information about local boat trips.

> **Open:** July and August, Mon to Sat, 9am to 1pm, 2pm to 7pm, Sun 10am to 1pm, 5pm to 7pm. Rest of year, Mon to Sat, 9am to noon, 2pm to 6pm.
> **Website:** www.ot-erdeven.fr – a good site. With English translation
> **Email:** ot.erdeven@wanadoo.fr

Situated to the south of the village, by the D781, are lines of standing stones which can still be wandered through at will. They are known as the **Alignment of Kerzerho** and there are ten rows of them.

Erdeven: Photo. M. S-Kellinghaus, CRTB

There are more than a thousand stones here. There are also four massive granite blocks or menhirs, two still standing, two fallen to the ground, these are the **Giants of Kerzerho**.

There is a 4 kilometre (2.5 mile) signposted walk from the town through the alignments.

At the **coast** at Erdeven the three beaches are excellent, with fine golden sand, stretching for 8 kilometres (about 5 miles): and they aren't crowded. **Kerhillio beach**, the largest and most southerly, is patrolled in July and August. Here canoes can be hired. The most northerly beach, **Kerminihy**, is where the nudists hang out. At **Etel**, further North (market day Tuesday), there is a marina, a fishing port and an oyster farming area (the wooden structures on which they are farmed are very distinctive).

11.2 Carnac

Population 4570. Market days, Wednesday and Sunday. Carnac has many restaurants and shops. It also has a long, good, beach.

There are two **Tourist Offices**, one in the town (74, avenue des Druides, 56342) and one at the beach. Here can be had a pamphlet about the area, with English sub sections, with an **outstanding map** of the local area, showing the 5 local beaches, roads and footpaths and the standing stones.

Open: 1st July to mid September, Monday to Saturday, 9.30am to 1pm, 2pm to 7pm, Sunday 10am to 1pm. Rest of September, closes between 12.30pm and 2pm, and all day Sunday. 1st to 30th June, Monday to Saturday 9.30am to 12.30pm, 2.30pm to 7pm, Sunday, 10am to 12.30pm.
Website: www.carnac.fr A good site, with English translation.
Email: accueiltourisme@carnac.fr

Carnac has 3000 standing stones. They are aligned in three main rows: the Ménec, the Kermario and the Kerlescan, in addition to groups of stone semi-circles. Visitors can climb a tall platform for the best view of the entire site. The Alignments have been fenced in to help vegetation growth, to stabilise the stones, but access is allowed in winter (November to March).

The following information about the megaliths is condensed from the excellent tourist board site at www.carnac.fr (English version). If you are especially keen on the subject, there is even more there...

Menec alignments
These alignments are the most representative of all three sites: 1165 metres long, 100 metres wide with a total of 1099 menhirs in 11 rows. The tallest stones are 4 metres high. The Menec alignments start in the South West with a cromlech composed of 71 rescued blocks, some of which are situated amongst the Menec village buildings.

Kermario alignments
The field is 1200 metres long and 100 metres wide with 1029 menhirs in 10 rows, some of the best specimens at Carnac. In Kermario, a large 3 metre high stone indicates the Manio tumulus as well as a dolmen on the road side. This dolmen was probably covered by an earth or stone tumulus when the menhirs were erected (around 5000 BC). Close by is a group of small menhirs, the quadrilatère du Manio and the Manio Giant, an impressive menhir over 6 metres high, the highest in the area.

Kerlescan alignments
This most western field is the smallest, but also the best preserved of all three sites. It comprises 555 menhirs in 13 rows, orientated East-West. At the western end of these alignments is a 39 stone cromlech (stone circle).

Kercado burial chamber and mound
Situated on private property, but open to the public (1€ honesty box), this structure is one of Brittany's rare dolmens still under its original cairn. Located south of the Kermario alignments, it is 30 metres in diameter and 5 metres high and crowned by a small menhir. The two pillars of the passage leading to the burial chamber, as well as the chamber's ceiling, bear the same designs found in other sites like Mané-Kerioned, petit Mont d'Arzon and Locmariaquer.

11.3 La Trinité sur Mer

Population 1500. Market days, Tuesday and Friday.

There are several good beaches here, with the main beach, the **Plage de Kervillen**, being patrolled in July and August. Lots of places to eat. There is also a fishing and pleasure port. Tourist Office: 30, cours des Quais, 56470. An excellent range of **free local maps**, including one which shows all of the standing stones in the Carnac area, as well as the beaches: and also 13 walking circuits, ranging from 4 km (2.5 miles) to 18km.

> **Open:** July and August, daily, 9am to 1pm, 2pm to 7pm. September to June, Monday to Saturday, 9am to noon, 2pm to 6pm.
> **Website:** www.ot-trinite-sur-mer.fr – in French only. Slow.
> **Email:** tourisme@ot-trinite-sur-mer.fr

11.4 Locmariaquer

The village is famed for its cultivation of oysters, with more than 40 enterprises producing over 3000 tons a year. The peninsula, which ends at Point Kerpenhir, offers several sheltered beaches and excellent coastal walks.

Menhir Brisé. Photo: A. Bobrovich, CRTB

Erdeven and Carnac

The area is internationally important for its birdlife, and very environmentally minded. At the western side of the straits of Morbihan, **Point Kerpenhir** offers a superb outlook over the inner and outer seas and the strait.

Tourist Office, 1 rue de la Victoire, 56740. Useful maps and some interesting brochures, most in French only.
   Open: July and August, 9am to 1pm, 2pm to 6pm. Rest of season, 10am to noon, 2pm to 6pm.

The peninsula boasts a great number of megaliths. The main site for standing stones (there are others, as the map from the tourist office shows) is the **Site Megalithique de Locmariaquer** in the north of the town. The site is well signposted and there is a large car park. The complex here has three major monuments.....

Le Grand Menhir Brisé
The broken stone here would have been the tallest in Brittany reaching 20.3m (60 feet!) and estimated to weigh 280 tons. It is among the largest of known stones to have been used by early man. It is also known as "Men er Hroeg" – the fairy's stone. It is composed of orthogneiss, the nearest occurrence of which is about 4km away, so transportation of this huge stone would have been a major feat 6000 years ago.

Le Tumulus de Er Grah
Just NW of the fallen stone is this 140m long mound that has been much restored. It is thought to have been constructed over one or two centuries and expanded to cover the original chamber after starting as a cairn and chamber then being extended in length.

La Table des Marchands
The low entrance faces SE and is just 1.3m (4ft) high, leading to a 7m (23ft) long passage that opens to a large round burial chamber about 3m (10ft) in diameter. It is covered by a carved capstone that measures 6.5x4m and weighs around 40 tons.
   Open: July and August, daily, 10am to 7pm. May and June, daily, 10am to 6pm.   Rest of year, daily, 10am to 12.30pm, 2pm to 5.15pm.
   Cost: Adult - 5€. Aged 18 to 25 – 3.50€. Under 18 – free.

12. The Quiberon Peninsula

An Exhilirating Day Out

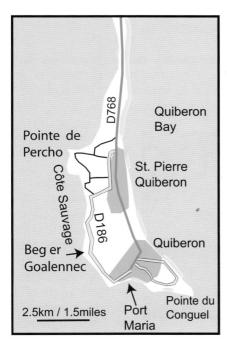

The presqu'île (peninsula) of Quiberon used to be an island, and even now is only joined to the mainland by a narrow strip of land, the road on which can become quite congested. Because of the popularity of the peninsula, it's best to visit on a weekday.

There is a train which runs in the summer from Auray to Quiberon town, but as the main attraction of the near-island is its wild and beautiful coastline, the trip is better made by car to allow greater freedom to explore. As a good part of the peninsula is built up, there are lots of cafes, restaurants and shops here.

12.1 St Pierre Quiberon

Market, Thursday morning.

There are 2 beaches here, both patrolled. (All of the beaches on the eastern side of the peninsula are good.) It's worth taking a look are the rows of 23 pre-historic standing stones, or Menhirs, near the church.

There is a **Tourist Office here**, in Rue Curie, 56510, in the middle of town, which has a **good free map of the peninsula**.
> **Open:** July and August, Mon to Sat, 9am to noon, 2pm to 7pm, Sunday, 10am to 1pm, 2pm to 5pm.

12.2 Quiberon
Quiberon. Population 5,000. Market, Saturday morning.

Market, Saturday morning. Quiberon is a popular seaside resort with all the attractions you'd expect, including a sheltered south facing beach, making it a jolly place to while away a few hours and enjoy an ice cream.

Quiberon. Photo: CRTB

Worth a visit while in the area is the **Belle Iloise** fish canning factory (Conserverie 'La Belle Iloise', Zone de Plein Ouest), which offers a guided tour, free, with a free tasting. La Belle Iloise is a bit of a tourist benefactor, as they supply many good local area maps, so I feel no guilt in quoting their own copy: 'Here we sell our products, produced with savoir-faire, and showered with praise from the gastronomic press, direct to the public. The 40 minute tour (in French) takes you back to 1932 and the beginnings of the enterprise and then to the factory of today'. Depending on the extent of your interest in fish preservation, you can also visit a fish smoker, the **Maison Lucas**, here, where they offer free guided tours and you can add to your lunch.

There is a **Tourist Office**, 14 Rue de Verdun, 56174 (near the south beach), which is open all year round. Here you will find an excellent handout map of the peninsula.

Open: July and August, daily, Mon to Sat, 9am to 1pm, 2pm to 7pm, Sunday, 10am to 1pm, 2pm to 5pm. Hours for rest of year not available at time of printing.
Website: www.quiberon.com which has an English version. This is a good site, giving, amongst other delights, a rather fine virtual pre-visit with panoramic views from a couple of lighthouses (phares).
Email: quiberon@quiberon.com

A drive to the east will take you past the institute of thalassotherapy (centre for seawater cures, a very big deal in France) to the **Pointe de Conguel** at the southern most tip of the peninsula, where there's a picnic spot with magnificent views. The point itself is a 15 minute walk from the parking area. There is a beach next to the parking area.

12.3   Boats go from Port Maria, Quiberon to…

(Park at 'la Siréne', 5 minute walk from booking office, 10€ a day)

Belle Isle 'The most beautiful Isle in Brittany'
This island is covered in another day out.

Houat Island (5 km / 3 miles long) 1 km wide
Population 380. See photo. This island has a wonderful coast, with high granite cliffs and a path around it. A paradise of peace and wild flowers, with 3 wonderful beaches, a port with several places to eat and shops (and bike hire). No cars. Very highly recommended. Crossings take 30 minutes or an hour and cost about 26€ return for an adult. It is essential to pre-book in high season. More information from the tourist office.

Hoedic Island (2.5km by 1km)
With a population of 150 and reached via Houat. The crossing takes about an hour and a half from Quiberon (same cost as Houat ticket). Reservation is essential in high season. The island has a nature reserve, of primary interest for its birds. It also has an old fort, where there are exhibitions on the flora and fauna of the island. There are three places to eat on the island.

Houat Island: Photo: H. Marcou, CRTB

12.4 The Wild Coast

Continue your clockwise exploration of the peninsula, and head towards the wild, western, coast – the **Côte Sauvage**. The coast drive is an excellent one, but to get the most out of the scenery it is better to explore on foot, weather permitting. Maps of routes for walks are available from the Quiberon tourist office. The coast on this side of the peninsula is stunning and varied, so you can enjoy a bracing walk along the cliffs, or visit one of the several tiny beaches, but the beaches are often pebbly and anyway **swimming is forbidden on this side of the coast**, as the waves are fierce even in calm weather. The movement of the sea has taken its toll on the coastline, and there are textbook examples of stacks and arches to marvel at. There are fine viewpoints at **Beg er Goalennec** and **Pointe de Percho**.

A Little History - The Battle of Quiberon Bay 21 November 1759

One of the British Royal Navy's greatest victories was won in Quiberon Bay in 1759, the 'wonderful year' of victories, immortalised in the song 'Hearts of Oak' composed to commemorate the battle.

France and Britain had been at war since 1756. France was doing badly, with her possessions in Canada, India and the West Indies either fallen or threatened. In Europe, she faced an alliance between Britain and Prussia. So the French planned to invade Britain, landing 20,000 troops in Scotland. The troop ships were guarded by 21 warships, commanded by Admiral Conflans.

The Royal Navy force of 23 warships, under Admiral Edward Hawke, caught the French fleet in Quiberon bay, where they had gone to embark the troops. Hawke chased the French into the bay under full sail and the leading group of British ships, commanded by Lord Howe, raced forward to engage the rearmost French. The British had better trained gunners and came off the best in the confusion that resulted, until Hawke, being afraid of being blown onshore, was forced to order his fleet to anchor late in the afternoon. The French fleet was routed, with five sunk and the flagship captured. At the loss of two British ships, the threatened invasion was defeated.

A reverse attempt, a landing from British ships, took place in 1795: but many of the soldiers who landed were French. They were 6,500 royalists, who, backed by 17,000 British troops, were intended to bring an end to the French revolution and restore the French monarchy. On landing, they were joined by 20,000 Breton peasants. The landings were commanded by two Counts, Puissaye and Hervilly. The antagonism between these two meant that the advance was delayed, thus giving their adversaries time to attack them. General Hoche and 13,000 troops trapped them in the Quiberon peninsula 'I have the royalist rats cooped up, and I'm at the door with my cats' he said. The royalists failed to break out and surrendered: the British ships being stopped by heavy seas from disembarking them.

All of the nobles who were captured were executed by firing squads at Auray and Vannes. Some peasants were spared, but nearly a thousand were shot just north of Auray, at a place which is called the field of the martyrs.

13. Belle Ile

The Beautiful Island

Belle Ile en mer (there is, oddly, also a Belle ile en Terre) is the largest of the Breton islands. Beautiful it certainly is. It has fine landscapes, wooded valleys falling to the turquoise sea, natural ports and fine sandy beaches. It also has some impressive cliffs (the highest point is at 63m – 200 feet). It has always been an attractive place for artists and remains so now. This is a good place to spend a day – or longer. There are lots of shops and restaurants on the island.

The two main ports are Le Palais (accessible by ferry from Quiberon) and Sauzon (accessible by ferry from Quiberon and Lorient, but less frequently – see 'how to get there'). The island is about 25 km by 9 km (16 miles by 6).

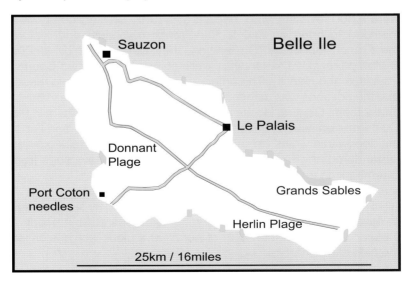

13.1 Le Palais - The Main Port

Tourist Office. Quai Bonnelle. (On the front, to the left of the landing stage). Post code 56360. The office provides an **excellent folding map of the island** with beaches, cycling routes and information. In English.

> **Open:** July and August, Monday to Saturday, 8.45am to 7.30pm, Sundays, 8.45am to 1pm. Rest of year, Monday to Saturday, 9am to 12.30pm, 2pm to 6pm.
> **Website:** www.belle-ile.com - a good site, which also has an English translation.

The Citadel in Le Palais, which now houses the island's museum, was built in 1549 and modified by Vauban (see entry on Vauban). It was a prison and barracks until 1961, when it was bought and restored by a wealthy couple. It can be visited (battlements, cells, museum).

> **Open:** 1st April to 31st October, daily, 9.30am to 6pm. Rest of year, closes for lunch (12pm to 2pm).
> **Cost:** Adult - 6.10€. Child (7 to 16) - 3.05€.

Le Palais town walls are a rare intact example of 19th century military architecture and a good place for a wander. There is an exhibition on the flora and fauna of the island (with several small aquariums) at the **Maison de la Nature**, within the town walls, not far from the tourist office.

> **Open:** 1st July to 31st August, Mon to Sat, 10.30am to 12.30pm, 3pm to 6.30pm. May, June and Sept, Tue to Sat, 10am to noon, 3pm to 6pm. Rest of year, Tue to Sat, 2pm to 6pm.
> **Cost:** Adult - 2€. Child (6 to 16) - 1€. Family - 5€.

Bikes can be hired from Le Palais (you will see the hire place when you get off the boat) for about 11€ per day. Maps of cycle routes and attractions are provided. This is a fine way to explore the island. There are 200km of cyclable trails, of which 35 km are specially signposted. Cars can also be hired here. There are 4 bus routes round the island. See the website, mentioned above, for times, or ask for a timetable from the tourist office.

13.2 Sauzon - Beloved of Artists

This, the second town of the island, is the most photographed and the most often portrayed in paintings. It is thought to derive its name from the presence of Saxons there. With its natural harbour, pink and white houses on the quayside and a lighthouse, it is an attractive spot. The coastal path to the headland at **Kerzo** (about 3 km), is beautiful, with a jagged shoreline, landslip and caves.

Sauzon. Photo: E. Speigelhalter - CRTB

13.3 Around the Island

The island has 102 km of pedestrian only coastal paths. If you are cycling, the **Port Coton needles**, about 10km (6 miles) from Le Palais, on the opposite side of the island, are worth a visit. These sea stacks get their name from the fact that the water foaming around their base looks like cotton wool. These atmospheric rocks were painted 36 times by Monet, in all weathers and light conditions.

Close by is the great lighthouse, of **Grand Phare**, which can sometimes be visited - 213 steps and an iron staircase. Not good if you suffer from vertigo, but giving an amazing view from Lorient to Croizic.

Port coton needles: J-P. Gratien, CRTB

There are many beaches around the island, from the small **Ramonette plage**, a few hundred yards south of Le Palais, to the large supervised **Grands Sables** (where kayaks and surf boards can be hired) and the smaller also supervised **Donnant** and **Herlin plages.**

A Little History

It is said that fairies, chased out of the forest of Broceliande (a remaining part of which is the Paimpont forest) were so sad at their expulsion that they wept and wept, producing the gulf of Morbihan. Into this sea they threw their crowns and the queen fairy's crown became Belle Isle.

The island, whose Breton name is Guerveur, was ruled for centuries by monks. Over the centuries it has been raided by all and sundry: Saxons, Normans, Dutch and English (the island being pillaged by the English for 3 weeks in 1572, and by the Dutch in 1674).

In 1763 the English once again seized the island, finally exchanging it for Minorca. Belle Isle saw an influx of French Canadians in 1766 who brought with them the potato, many years before it was introduced to France. They had been expelled from Canada after the English conquered that country. The island was once again occupied, by the Germans, in 1940, when many of the inhabitants were expelled.

How to get there

Ferries run from **Quiberon to Le Palais** up to 13 times a day in the high season, 7 times a day in low season. The tourist office recommends pre-booking for foot passengers. Reservations can be made at the tourist office or at the shipping office of the ferry company, SMN. The ferries also take cars, but for cars, reservation is essential. The crossing takes 45 minutes.

> **Cost:** (foot passengers) Adult - 14€. Age 4 to 24 – 8.50€. Age 3 and under - 1€. **Website:** www.smn-navigation.fr - also in English.

In high season there is also a fast motorboat (20 minute crossing) between Quiberon and Le Palais, for foot passengers only. (There are also **boats to Sauzon** from both Quiberon and Lorient in high season, for foot passengers. However there is only one from Lorient and two from Quiberon each day).

14. Pont Aven and Area

Painters, Devils and Bees

14.1 Pont Aven - Town of Painters

Pont Aven. Population 3,000. Market, Tuesday morning.

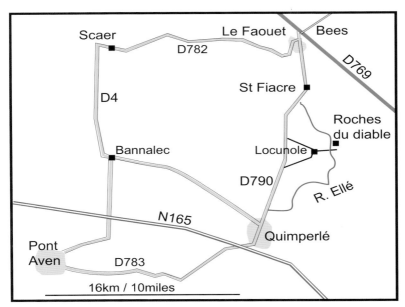

This town is an important spot in the history of art, for in 1886 Paul Gaugin came to paint here - he stayed in one of the small inns, now the Maison de la Presse. Around Gaugin, Charles Laval, Charles Filiger, Ferdinand du Puigaudeau and Emile Bernard grew up the School of Pont Aven, paintings of country scenes of often superb luminosity. The town remains an important artists' colony to this day.

As well as the many shops and commercial galleries, there is a **Museum and art gallery** (the gallery has 4 rooms) which always has interesting exhibitions, with 50 to 60 paintings of the Pont Aven school on show at any one time.

Open: Everyday from 10am to 12.30pm, 2pm to 6.30pm.
Cost: Adult - 4€. Child (ages 12 to 20) - 2.50€. Under 12's - free.

Tourist Office, 5 place de l'Hôtel de Ville. 29930. One of their brochures has a map of the town, and a map of 3 pleasant walks, of an hour to an hour and a half, along the river and through the woods.

Open: July and August, daily, 9.30am to 7.30pm (at other periods and bank holidays, it is closed between noon and 2pm).
Website: www.pontaven.com - partly translated into English.
Email: ot.pont.aven@wanadoo.fr

When walking in the town, it is interesting to look up. Often there are windows just under the roofs, especially on **rue Emile Bernard**. These are the studios that were converted for the painters by home owners.

A Little History

Pont Aven was once known as 'the town with fourteen mills and fifteen houses'. It was a prosperous place boasting twelve fairs each year. In the 18th century, locals complained that on Tuesdays it took an hour longer than usual to cross the town due to all the people. Then the port was built and trade was carried on as far afield as England. As the coastal trade declined, Pont Aven did not nod off to sleep, as so many other small ports did. It was saved by its beauty. In the 1860's, American painters settled there, to be followed by hundreds of fellow artists from all over the world, among them, as mentioned above, Paul Gauguin. Gauguin took up painting late, having been a sailor and later a stock broker.

Abandoning his wife and 5 children (nice fellow), he took up painting full time at the age of 38. He made 6 visits to Pont Aven and nearby **Pouldu**. It was here, under the influence of the painter Émile Bernard, that Gauguin turned away from impressionism and adapted a less naturalistic style, which he called synthetism.

14.2 Quimperlé – The Double Town

Maison des Archers,
Quimperle, Guegan, CRTB

Population 11,000. The main market is all day Friday, although the market hall is open Tuesday to Friday mornings (fruit, vegetable and fish).

Quimperlé describes itself as a 'double town' as it has two centres, one, the low town, on an island between two rivers, the other, the high town, on the west bank of the river. The two centres are linked by roads and two steep, stepped, streets.

A pleasant town (or two!) to wander round, with its rivers, 2 interesting old churches, some fine buildings, the medieval Floral Bridge and a pretty riverside public garden with picnic tables. It has a good selection of shops, including three supermarkets.

Tourist Office, 45, Place Saint-Michel (high town), 29300. Excellent, free, town maps.
> **Open:** July and August, Mon to Sat, 9.30am to 7pm, Sunday 10am to noon.Rest of year, Mon to Sat, 9am to 12.30pm, 2pm to 6pm.
> **Email:** ot.quimperle@wanadoo.fr

14.3 The Devil's Rocks

Take the D790 north until you see **Locunole** signposted (about 3 miles). Go through Locunole, then left after the bridge. The **Roches du Diable** are signposted near a carpark. A pleasant 30 minute walk above the river Ellé. Paths lead to the top of the Devil's Rocks which drop vertically to the river. The rocks are a popular place for white water canoeing, kayaking, rafting, or for a walk and a picnic.

14.4 St Fiacre - Sins In Wood

A pleasant little hamlet with an almost English feel. A fine chapel with a sometimes witty, carved screen dating from 1480, showing examples of sin and bad behaviour (look for the man vomiting a fox - drunkenness). A little gem.

St Fiacre. J.P. Gratien, CRTB

14.5 Bees (And Ants)

Kercadoret, 56320, on the D769 just north of Le Faouët. L'Abeille Vivante et La Cite des Fourmis. The living bee and the city of the ants – a bit of a mouthful but my favourite attraction in the whole of Brittany! Traditional bee hives of several countries, exotic (TV shaped for example) hives, bees swarming, honey collection – if it's bees, it's here. Also a huge enclosed wood ants' nest that you can enter through a Perspex tunnel (if you're small). Just magical. With a shop selling wax and honey.

Website: www.abeilles-et-fourmis.com (French and Breton only) Open: July and August, daily, 10am to 7pm. Low season, 10am to 12.30pm, 2pm to 6pm. With English audio commentary available. Handicapped access. **Cost:** Adult - 6€. Child (4 to 15 years) - 4€.

14.6 Le Faouët

Market days – 1st and third Wednesday of the month.

Many artists in the nineteenth century visited Le Faouët for its remoteness and preserved costumes and traditions: an essential staging post on the trail of Breton exoticism. A small town with shops and eating places, it is mainly notable for its 16th century covered **market hall** and its beautiful surroundings (both the rivers Scorff and Ellé are very beautiful and have fine walks beside them). **Tourist Office**, 3 rue des cendres, 56320. Distribute a good range of free guides in English, and local maps.

> **Open:** All year. July and Aug, Mon to Sat, 10am to 12.30pm, 2pm to 6.30pm.
> Sept to June, Tue to Sat, 10am to 12.30pm, 2pm to 5.30pm.
> **Website:** www.paysroimorvan.com
> **Email:** officedetourisme.lefaouet@wanadoo.fr

Musée de Faouet, 1 rue de Quimper, 56320. About 400 works in 6 rooms, consisting of items of local history and paintings of the area between 1845 to 1945. The staff are friendly and speak English, and there are generally some fine paintings.

> **Open:** Daily, 10am to noon, 2pm to 6pm. Cost: Adult - 4€. Child (10 to 12) - 1.55€. Under 10 - Free.
> **Email:** museedufaouet@wanadoo.fr

14.7 Bannalec - Artistic Inspiration

Two nineteenth century painters, Camille Bernier (1823-1902) and Vincent Vidal (1811-1889), loved Bannalec. Bernier, an admirer of Corot with whom he had studied, was considered by his contemporaries to be the artistic ambassador of Brittany. From 1860 until his death he painted mostly the heaths, woods, sunken roads and fields around Bannalec. Some of his works can be seen at the galleries in Morlaix and Quimper.

15. Concarneau

Fortress by the Sea

Population 20,000

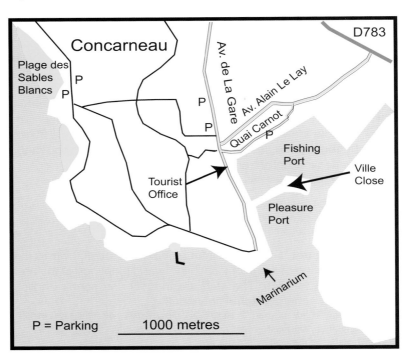

P = Parking   1000 metres

The daily indoor market offers fresh fish, shell fish and fruit and vegetables. There is also an open air market in front of the **Ville Close** on Mondays and Fridays (8am until 1pm). And there is a fish auction – an interesting place to start the day if you are an early riser - the auction usually starts at 6.30am, when the fishermen (who set out at midnight) return.

Concarneau has a lot to offer. The beauty of the place is reason enough to visit, but there are a number of other diversions. Unsurprisingly, this being the third largest fishing port in France, most are related to the sea.

The town really has two hearts - one historical and the other nautical and financial, in the port. There are lots of fine restaurants in Concarneau, many of them overlooking the sea. If you eat seafood in one of them, chances are it will have been landed here earlier in the day. The port's size and importance don't mean that it isn't very attractive and visitor-friendly. In the mid 19th to mid 20th centuries it was very popular with painters, and the artistic and seafaring communities were to some degree symbiotic- the boats gave the artists something to paint - while in 1905, when the sardine shoals moved away from the area, the artists organised aid for the impoverished fishermen and their families. The historic part of town, the **Ville Close**, is within the walls.

The **Tourist Office**, Quai de l'Aguillon, 29900, has a very useful free leaflet in English about the town, which has a good map.
Open: July and August, 9am to 7pm. Rest of year, 9am to noon, 2pm to 6pm. **Website:** www.tourismeconcarneau.fr - very slow, wholly in French **Email:** otsi.concarneau@wanadoo.fr

A **"Little Train"** goes round Concarneau (departs from opposite the Ville Close). This is a guided tour on the history of fishermen, canneries and painters. (In French. A leaflet in English is provided). The train runs along the promenade, with splendid views across to the Glenan islands. The tour takes 35/40 minutes.
Runs: From 1st April to 30th September, daily from 10.30am to 6pm, according to the demand (the train leaves with a minimum of 6 passengers).
Cost: Adult - 4.50€. Child (under 18) - 3.50€. Under 5 - free.

Concarneau

The Marinarium has the worthy mission statement : 'Knowing, understanding, managing the sea ...and showing it greater respect.' The Marinarium is the showcase of the marine biology station and explains the importance of the oceans and their extraordinary biodiversity. Local marine flora and fauna are shown in a large 120,000 litre pool.

> **Open:** July and Aug, daily, 10am to 7pm. April, May, June and Sept, daily, 10am to noon, 2pm to 6pm. Feb and March, 2pm to 6pm but closed Mondays.
> **Cost:** Adult - 5€. Child (6 to 12) - 3€. Under 6 – free.

Photo: J-P. Gratien, CRTB

The **Ville Close**, with narrow cobbled and ancient streets, is one of the most visited tourist destination in Brittany. To access the ramparts, turn left after the second bridge upon entering the Ville Close. There is a small charge for this in-season. The ramparts give great views of the walled town, the sea and the extra-muros (they slip into Latin round here for some reason 'muros' means walls, 'extra' is outside).

The Musée de la Pêche, 3, Rue Vauban, Ville-close. The fishing museum is housed in the Arsenal building, which has also served as a barracks and a fishing school. It tells the history of Concarneau, as well as explaining the fishing techniques used in the area, with diagrams and models. Various types of boat are on display, some models, some real, all interesting. You can go aboard the Hemerica, a 100 foot (34m) trawler and explore her from stem to stern.

The evolution of the waters around Concarneau is also explored, and the effect that these changes had on the town - the disappearance of sardines, for example. Look out for the coelacanth, a species of fish that has been around for 300 million years.

Open: July and August, 9.30am to 8pm. Rest of year, 10am to noon, 2pm to 6pm.
Cost: Adult - 6€. Child (6 to 12) - 4€. Under 6 – free.

Every year Concarneau hosts the wonderful **Fête des Filets Bleus**, a festival of Breton music, costume and dance. The first was held in 1905 as a fundraiser for the sailors affected by the loss of sardines. It takes place on the weekend of the penultimate Sunday in August, and if you're in the area at this time, be sure to go.

There are several safe and sandy **beaches** near and in the town.

A Little History

Concarneau's life as a settlement began in the 4th Century A.D, when a religious community grew up, peopled by the faithful who were attracted to the site because of its beauty, isolation and superb defensive position. They settled on the small island which is the 'Ville Close' (walled town) of today. In contrast to its religious beginnings, Concarneau later became a retreat for those fleeing the law.

The magnificent granite ramparts you can see today were built in the 14th and 15th centuries to replace the previous fortifications. During the Wars of Religion the town was taken by surprise by the Calvinists, but the Royal troops succeeded in repelling them, and because of this King Henry IV received the keys to the city in 1594. In the 17th Century, Louis XIV instructed Vauban (see entry on Vauban) to carry out some work on the defences of the Ville Close, which he duly did, and the results can be seen today, particularly in the castle built to overlook its entrance.

As well as the garrison, Concarneau consisted of a population of fishermen who worked on the trawlers and who traded in wheat and wine.

The fish was pressed, dried and sent by horse and cart to the inland towns. In 1795, 300 fishing boats were recorded but this relative affluence was stopped short by war with Britain and the coastal blockades. The first canning factories appeared in 1851 so that the standard of living increased and in 1900 records showed 30 factories employing 2,000 workers (out of a population of 7,000).

The disappearance in 1905 of the large shoals of sardines brought major trouble for the fleet of 800 trawlers. The "Filets Bleus" Charity was founded during this period to assist the fisherman's families who were most in need. During the German occupation, large trawlers sheltering from Boulogne and Lorient marked the beginning of a generation of specifically designed deep-sea ships. Fishing regulations, the cost of fuel, foreign competition and the evolution of tastes were to provoke a new crisis resulting in the closure of factories. In consequence the local economy diversified to rapidly send fresh fish towards the larger areas of consumption. Today, the port activity turns towards shipbuilding and repairing.

Boat trips

Fishing aboard the **Santa-Maria**. A half day fishing trip with a guaranteed catch (how they do that is anyone's guess). The Santa-Maria is a converted sardine-boat. Rod and bait are provided, but a waterproof jacket, a knife and something to hold the fish is necessary.

Times: July and August, Monday to Friday, from the harbour. Ask for times at the tourist office.
Cost: Adult - 35€. Child (under 12) -20€.

Deep sea fishing is also available (a long trip, noon to 10pm)
Times: Enquire at the tourist office.
Cost: 80€ a person - food not provided.

Boat trips to the Glenan Islands
Times: ask at the tourist office.
Cost: Adults - 28€. Child (4 to 12) - 14.50€. Under fours - 4.50€.

16. Quimper and Area

In Gradlon's Kingdom

16.1 Quimper

Population 65,000. There is a daily food market in the Halles St-François.

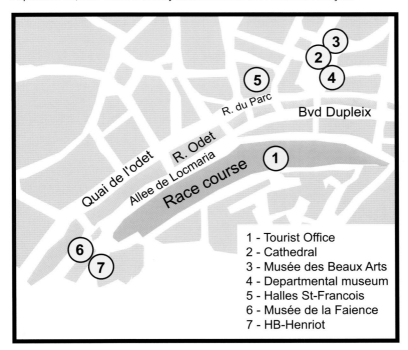

1 - Tourist Office
2 - Cathedral
3 - Musée des Beaux Arts
4 - Departmental museum
5 - Halles St-Francois
6 - Musée de la Faience
7 - HB-Henriot

Quimper is a beautiful city, with a strong Breton character, most keenly felt in the pedestrianised area of Vieux Quimper, where half-timbered buildings house creperies and shops sell traditional Breton goods. The town is well worth a visit, especially when the Festival of Cornouaille takes place towards the end of July. The biggest event of its kind in Europe, it is dedicated to popular arts and traditions.

Locals dress in their best Breton garb, the women wearing their coiffes, the distinctive lace head-dresses of the region, and there is much waving of flags and banners, music from bagpipes, bombard and harp, and reciting of poetry in the Breton language.

The town is situated at the meeting place, or confluence, of the rivers Odet and Steir, as the Breton name Kemper (confluence) suggests. There are fine walks along the river here. The area of Locmaria, south of the river, has shops and a museum of porcelain, which is a speciality of the town. There is also a rather fine garden, le **Jardin de la Retraite** (closed Sunday), just north of the cathedral, as well as plenty of other green spaces and parks in the town. There is a 'petit train' that runs round the town, starting near the museums.

Photo: J.P. Gratien, CRTB

The **Tourist Office**, Place de la Résistance, 29000, provides a useful map of the city.

> **Open:** High season 9am to 7pm, except Sunday: 10am to 1pm, 3pm to 6pm. Rest of year, 9.30am to 12.30pm, 1.30pm to 6pm (closed Sunday).
> **Website:** www.quimper-tourisme.com
> **Email:** contact@quimper-tourisme.com

The **Cathedral of Saint Corentin** is a fine example of Gothic architecture, combining both Parisian and Norman influences. It is the earliest Gothic cathedral in lower Brittany, as it was begun in 1240. The twin towers, which dominate the town, are much newer, dating from 1856. To pay for these 76 metre (235 feet) wonders, a tax was imposed on the diocese of one sou per person per year, which became known as the 'sou of Corentin' - Corentin being the saint to whom the cathedral, and city, are dedicated. He was a holy hermit whom King Gradlon encountered when hunting one day and whom he appointed as bishop. Much of the interior was destroyed after the revolution, but the two ton altar is worthy of note, as are the tombstones in the floor.

A joint ticket exists for all the 4 attractions mentioned below. It is available at any of the attractions and cost about 75% of the total admission price for the 4.

The **Musée des Beaux Arts**, 40 Place St Corentin (opposite the Cathedral) is a cracker. The best art museum in the area, the collection is strong on late 19th century and early 20th century art and demonstrates how visiting artists perceived Brittany and its residents, perpetuating a romantic view of the area. Breton mythology is also represented with Evariste Luminais' interpretation of Ys (see Myths and Legends of Brittany).
Open: 2nd week July to early September, daily, 10am to 7pm. Low season, 10am to noon, 2pm to 6pm daily, except Tuesday.
Cost: Adult - 4€. Between the ages of 12 and 26 - 2.50€. Under 12 - free.

Musée Départemental Breton (opposite the cathedral). The departmental museum is housed in the ex-palace of the Bishops of Cornouaille, which dates back to the 15th century. Displays on the history of the area, from the Iron Age to the 1930's. With traditional costumes, furniture and wood engravings.
Open: June to September, daily, 9am to 6pm. Rest of year, 9am to noon, 2pm to 5pm, closed Sunday morning and all day Monday.
Cost: Adult - 3.80€. Under 18 - free.

Musée de la faience. For 300 years Quimper has produced high quality decorated porcelain. The museum displays 500 of its total collection of 2000 pieces, with works inspired by religion, history, myths and legends, and daily life. There is a shop and guided tours. English speaking tours can be arranged.

> **Open:** From mid April to mid October, Mon to Sat, 10am to 6pm (closed bank holidays).
> **Cost:** Adult - 4€. Young (18 to 25) - 2.60€. Children - 2.30€. Under 7 – free.

La Faïencerie HB-Henriot. A working pottery (since 1690) producing high quality porcelain. The 'petit Breton' which so often features was a 19th century invention, a stylised image of a typical Breton peasant which rapidly gained popularity. Guided visits in English and French

> **Open:** Monday to Friday (and Saturday, in July and Aug).
> **Cost:** Adult - 3.50€. Children (8 to 14) - 2€. Under 8 – free.

Photo: CRTB

Shopping

The lanes leading off the cathedral square are a treasure trove of fascinating boutiques, modern and traditional shops are side by side in the half-timbered buildings. As Quimper is one of the finest places in Brittany to sample cider and crepes, it would be a shame not to do so.

A Little History

Dating from at least Roman times, in later times Quimper was the home of the Count of Cournaille, whose descendants became the Dukes of Brittany. From the 13th century, the construction of the present cathedral and ramparts defined the town. In tradition, the city became the seat of power of King Gradlon of Cournaille after his mythical city of Ys was submerged (see Brittany of myth and legend).

16.2 Parc Odet Leisure Park, Elliant

Seven hectares (17 acres) of walks and relaxation in a landscaped valley beside a lake: ball pool, bouncy castle, trampoline, monkey bridge, cable slide, pedalos, rowing boats, giant billiards, picnic areas (outdoor and sheltered), a bar and ice creams.

Open: July & August, 11am to 7pm. Otherwise, from April to end October, Wednesdays, Saturdays and Sundays, 2pm to 7pm.
Cost: Over 3's and adults – 6.50€. Age 3 and under – free.
Website: www.odet-loisirs.com (in French only).

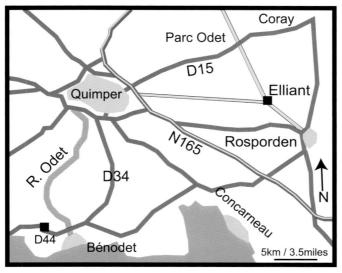

16.3 Bénodet – A Lovely Seaside Resort

Population 2800. Market, Monday, morning only.

A charming seaside resort at the mouth of the Odet, Bénodet being the Breton for "tip of the Odet". Because the river is navigable as far as Quimper, throughout the middle ages Bénodet was used as the commercial outer harbour for Quimper, with produce from the town and surrounding countryside being carried down the river then transferred to coasters to be shipped to countries such as Spain, England and the Netherlands. There are excellent beaches here.
Bénodet's renaissance began at the start of the last century when sea bathing became very fashionable, as did excursions in small boats. Bénodet's charms, combining the gentleness of its river with the harsh ocean have given it a special atmosphere that has been enjoyed by generations of visitors. Boats can be taken from here to explore the river Odet and the Glenan islands.

Tourist office: 29, avenue de la Mer, 29950. Useful brochures of the area, with versions in English.
Open: Mid June to mid Sep, Mon to Sat, 9am to 7pm, Sun, 10am to 6pm. Rest of year, Mon to Sat, 9.30am to noon, 2pm to 5pm.
Website: www.benodet.fr - with version in English. A good site.
Email: tourisme@benodet.fr

16.4 Combrit Botanical Garden

The **Botanical Garden of Cornouaille** has 4 hectares (10 acres) of gardens and over 3,500 plant species, including Japanese and Indian varieties. Plants for sale. There is also a geological museum, which is included in the admission price.
Open: Daily, from March to late November. July and Aug, 10am to 7pm. Rest of season, 10am to noon, 2pm to 7pm.
Cost: (Park and museum): Adult - 6€. Child - 3€.

17. Locronan to Raz Point

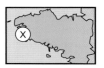

A Day out in Cornouaille

In ancient times **Cornouaille** was a kingdom which extended over much of what is now Finistère and part of what is now Morbihan. It got its name because it had been settled by members of the Cornovii tribe of Wales. Probably the county of Cornwall, in England, got its name for the same reason. Cornouaille became a county and a bishopric in Medieval times. Nowadays it is the area around Quimper, which is its chief town.

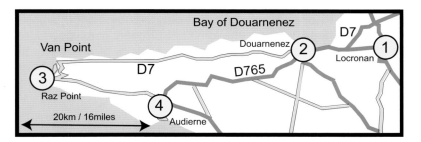

17.1   Locronan – A Druidic Survival

Locronan. Population 800.

Locronan is a a very attractive small, granite town of historical interest. It is named after an Irish missionary Saint Ronan (Locus Ronani, Ronan's place). Many films have been shot here, including "Tess" directed by Roman Polanski. Locronan has become a very arty place – painters, weavers, potters and tanners have all set up shop here. There are plenty of places to eat.

The **Tourist Office**, place de la Mairie, 29180, provides a small leaflet about the town in English with a useful map. Attached to the tourist office, there is a small **Museum**, with 100 paintings (Painters discover Brittany 1900 – 1950), as well as exhibitions on the history and old crafts of Locranon.

> **Open:** (tourist office. and museum) July to Aug, daily, except Sat morning, 10am to 1pm, 2pm to 7pm. April to June, Mon to Fri, 10am to noon, 2pm to 6pm.
> **Cost:** (museum): Adult - 2€. Under 12 – free.
> **Website:** www.locronan.org - In French only.
> **Email:** locronan.tourisme@wanadoo.fr

The **Grande Place** (great square) is surrounded by a superb group of 14 **houses dating** from the 17th to 19th centuries. These include **the Bureau des toiles** and the **Hôtel de la Compagnie des Indes**. The **Priory church**, built between 1420 and 1480, adjoins **Le Pénity chapel** where is the tomb of St Ronan. It is a good idea to leave the square and visit the small network of pretty streets which are also full of old houses. When you reach the **Notre-Dame chapel** (15th to 17th Century) stop to look at the modern stained-glass windows by Alfred Manessier.

Locronan - Photo: M. S-Kellinghaus, CRTB

The **Troménies**, which are religious pardons (see entry on religion), have made Locronan famous. The **Petite Troménie** takes place every year on the second Sunday in July, and follows the 6 km (3.75 mile) journey that St. Ronan took every morning.

The **Grande Troménie**, which takes place every 6 years, follows the 12 kilometre (7.5 mile) journey which St. Ronan made every week, with 12 pauses to read the Gospel. The schedule for them is 2001, 2007, 2013, 2019….

The story behind the 12 pauses of the Grande Troménie is quite remarkable, linking the Christian faith with a much older one. The Celts, under their druid priests, created large sacred areas, called Nemeton. The sacred function of the Nemeton was to represent on earth the movement of the stars in the sky. The Locranon **Nemeton**, which still survives, has a perimeter of a dozen kilometres, with twelve key points, representing the twelve months, and gods, of the Celtic year. The reason that the Nemeton at Locranon still survives in its original form – the only one in Europe to do so – is because it was incorporated into the Christian faith by Saint Ronan. Instead of trying to destroy the Nemeton, Ronan merely replaced the Druidic divinities with Christian saints – so Ana became Ann, while Lug became ….Ronan. During the Grande Troménie, when the remains of Saint Ronan are paraded around the Nemeton, the twelve pauses are at the points where the druids worshipped their gods.

The sailcloth industry brought riches to the town from the 15th century (the sails of the Spanish Armada fleet came from here). Locronan underwent a period of decline from the 17th century. Its commercial activity grew again in the second half of the 20th century.

Above the town is **Mount Locronan**. This (289m/948 ft.) hill has a magnificent view of the bay of Douarnenez, the Cap de la Chèvre and the Menez Hom. Standing on it, the chapel of Ar Zonj, dedicated to St. Ronan, is one of the stopping places of the Troménie.

The **Nevet Forest**, 228ha (563 acres) of beech, oak and chestnut trees is an ideal place to go walking. Guides (in French) available at the tourist office.

17.2   Douarnenez and the Port Museum

There is an open market on the mornings of Monday and Saturday – and a covered one every morning in the market hall.

The **Tourist Office**, 1, rue du Dr Mével, 29100, provides a good brochure, in English **'Walks around Douarnenez'** (3 walks, about 2 hours each) as well as a good, free, 20 page pamphlet, in English, covering the local area, Cornouaille.
> **Open:** July to Aug, daily 10am to 7pm. Other months, 10am to noon, 2pm to 5pm or 6pm, closed Sunday.
> **Website:** www.douarnenez-tourisme.com - in French only.
> **Email:** tourisme.douarnenez@wanadoo.fr

Douarnenez is a great centre for fishing and canning, handling mackerel, shell fish and sardines. The port, clustered at the base of one of the finest bays in the world, has a picturesque and lively front and five good beaches. On Tristan island, just offshore (accessible only at low tide), the Romans used to make a very popular fish paste. More romantically, it is where, in Arthurian legend, Tristan and Isolde are buried under two interlacing trees. The bay is the site of the legendary city of Ys. For more on both of these subjects, see the entries in 'Legendary Brittany'. Douarnenez attracts sailors, painters, poets and those who love character and the sea. It's motto is typically Breton: "Dalc'h Mad!", Hold fast!

The **Port museum** is set in a floating harbour where you can visit five boats. There are also exhibitions of marine life, wooden boats, sailing ships and the fishing industry. The museum does not have a restaurant or café.
> **Open:** Mid June to mid Sep, daily, 10am to 7pm. Spring (end march to mid June) and autumn (mid to end September), open every day, except Monday, 10am to 12.30pm, 2pm to 6pm.

Cost: Adult - 6.20€. Child - 3.80€. Under 6 - free. (These prices are for the museum and the 5 boats. Just one or other of them is a little cheaper). **Website:** www.port-musee.org - In French only. Rather slow.

17.3 The Pointe de Raz

This famous headland is 72 metres (200 feet) above sea level, with superb coastal views, especially over the Isle de Sein (see next entry).

The (pay) parking area, from which one walks to the headland, is quite touristy, with cafes and shops. A walk around the headland reveals the sheer gullies in the cliff face, into one of which – the **Enfer de Plogoff** (inferno of Plogoff) the waves crash deafeningly. Out to sea, the headland dips down in a series of islets, on the last of which is perched the **Vieille lighthouse**. On clear days, two other lighthouses can be seen. To the north is a popular surfing beach (sand and pebbles).

Pointe de Raz. Photo: G. Fisher, CRTB

17.4   The Isle de Sein - Heroic Island

The island (Enez Sun in Breton) is less than 1 square kilometre (0.5 square mile) in size, low-lying (the highest point is 6 metres, mean height 1.5 metres) and has been submerged twice. It has one village, which has narrow alleys to protect from the wind. There are about ten bars, cafes, restaurants and two food shops on the island.

Given the practical difficulties in getting to it (you often have to book the ferry several days ahead and in high season, the restaurants too), the island will probably be visited mostly in print: but it is a place which is certainly worth knowing about.

Often shrouded in fog, as often torn by winds, it is a very hard place, which has until recently lived wholly from the sea, breeding very tough people. The harshness of the island's environment is recognised by the government - the islanders pay no property taxes. A mysterious place, shrouded in mists and antiquity. Sacred to the Druids, it is first recorded by Pomponius Mela in the first century AD. "The Isle de Sein in the British Sea is famous for the oracle of a Gaulish god, whose priestesses, living in the holiness of perpetual virginity, are said to be nine in number. The Gauls call them Senae and believe them to be endowed with extraordinary gifts, to rouse the seas and the wind by their incantations, to turn themselves into whatsoever animal form they may choose, to cure diseases which among others are incurable, to know what is to come and to foretell it." It is sometimes believed to be Avalon, the island where Arthur sleeps (but being devoid of trees, apple or otherwise, this seems unlikely).

It could be called the bravest place in France. Apart from its tradition of life saving, there is its war record. After the German triumph at Dunkirk, in 1940, when Britain was thrown from the continent and France surrendered, the leader of the Free French army, General De Gaulle, broadcast from London to the French people asking for patriotic French men to join him to fight the German invaders.

The entire male population of the Isle de Sein sailed to England to join him, prompting De Gaulle to ask when reviewing his 600 volunteers and finding half of them were from the island: "What is the Isle de Sein half of France then?" A quarter of the male population of the island died on the battlefield. De Gaulle visited the island after the war. He told the islanders that France owed them a great debt and asked them what they wished in return. The islanders simply asked for a daily link with the mainland. The wish was granted, and to this day there is a daily boat service.

Getting There

It is wise to book your tickets ahead, as the ferries are often full in season.

The ferries: (the companies are Penn ar Bed & Vedettes Biniou) run from Audierne.

Crossings: In July and August there are 4 return crossings per day. From September to June, there is a daily crossing at 9.30am (but verify this time), except on Wednesdays, returning from the island at 4pm. The crossing takes 1 hour.

Cost: Return price from Audierne about 25€ (adult), 14€ (3 to 15). Under 3, free. (there is also a Sunday service in season from Brest and Camaret)

Websites: www.vedettebiniou.freesurf.fr and www.penn-ar-bed.fr

17.5 Audierne

A fishing port on the estuary of the Goyen. There is a beach a mile from the town, near the pier where the boats go to Sein. There is a fish farm with pools full of shellfish (crabs, lobsters and prawns). The **Tourist Office** is open during the summer from 10am to 12.30pm and 2.30pm to 7pm daily.

Website: www.audierne-tourisme.com
Email: ot.audierne@wanadoo.fr

There is an **Aquarium**. Allow roughly two and a half hours for the visit. 200 species of fish, shellfish, and sharks. The sea birds can be seen feeding (including cormorants diving under water). It has a restaurant overlooking the bay and gift shop.

Open: daily between 1st April and 30th September, 10am to 7pm.
Cost: Adult - 11.50€. Child (4 to 14) - 8.50€. Family (2 adults, 3 children) – 41.50€.
Website: www.aquarium.fr - In French only, rather slow.

The Crozon Peninsula

18. The Crozon Peninsula

Bulwark against Sea and Man

The Crozon Peninsula thrusts out into the Atlantic south of Brest. On the coast there are towering cliffs, often surmounted by defence works against France's historical maritime enemies, the English, Dutch and Spanish: not to mention the odd German pillbox. Inland are moorland uplands. Part of the Armorique National Park, this is a dramatic, fascinating and often beautiful area.

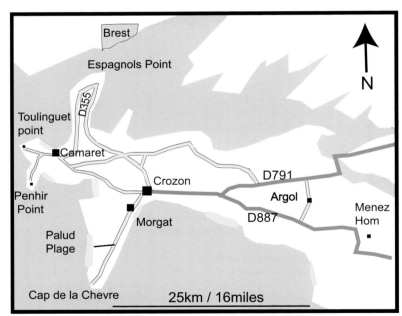

18.1 Ménez Hom - A Fine Viewpoint

A good way to start the journey around the peninsula, visibility permitting, is to go to the heights of Ménez-Hom, a hill of 330 metres (1,082 ft), an outrider at the west end of the Noire Mountains.

This hill, with its characteristic remains of German anti-aircraft emplacements, is one of the great Breton viewpoints, giving views over the peninsula, the bays of Brest (to the right) and the sweep of its roadstead right up to St Mathieu's point. To the left is the Bay of Douarnenez culminating at Van Point. Between these two is spread out the Crozon Peninsula itself. In the legend of Tristan and Isolde (see Legendary Brittany) this hill is associated with Mark, the third member of the love triangle on which Wagner based his opera. Mark, King of Cornwall who ruled at Tintagel, is supposedly buried on the side of the hill. He will not reach paradise until the day when, perched on his tomb, he is able to see the clock tower of the church of Sainte-Marie du Ménez-Hom. An interesting myth (which has echoes in one told of the Rollright Stones in Oxfordshire), presumably to do with the Christianisation of the area. From the hill, continue west on the D887. Argol, just off the road, has a folk museum (closed at lunchtime) a bar, a restaurant and a rather fine parish close (see Religious Brittany).

18.2   Crozon / Morgat - A Superb Beach

Crozon and Morgat are joined, with Morgat being the more attractively situated of the two. There are 2 **Tourist offices** here, it is worth visiting either. Their little brochure in English even includes a couple of recipes. The seasonal **Tourist office at Morgat** is in the Place d'Ys.
Open: July and August, daily, 10am to 1pm, 3pm to 7.30pm.

Main tourist office at Crozon is in the Bd de Pralognan. (29160)
Open: July and August, daily, 9.15am to 1pm, 2pm to 7pm. Rest of year from Monday to Saturday, 9.15am to noon, 2pm to 5.30pm.
Website: www.crozon.com

The main street of **Morgat**, with its cheerful and colourful facades, runs along a beautiful azure bay. Here are many restaurants, bars and cafes (and a supermarket). The beach is excellent and slopes gently into the pristine water, with a beautiful view across the bay to the cliffs opposite.

There is a well-sheltered harbour full of pleasure boats. From here can be taken a 45 minute tour across the bay to the caves on the opposite shore, accessible only by sea but with steep chimneys up to the cliff tops. Three rival boat companies run these trips from the quay, setting off every quarter of an hour in high season (May to September). The boats often leave full, so it's worth booking a few hours in advance. Kayaks can also be hired here (2 seater, 3 hours, around 20€) and bikes (around 10€ a day).

18.3   La Palud Beach

La Palud is a fine beach (popular with surfers but not suitable for swimming). From Morgat follow the roadsigns to "Cap de la Chèvre", on the D255. Go through the hamlet of Montourgar (before getting to the Cap de la Chèvre), turn right at the next crossroads. From there, follow the road to La Palud. After you have passed through the hamlet of La Palud (bumpy track), there is a carpark on top of the dunes.

18.4   Cap de la Chèvre (goat's cape)

Interesting geologically (there is a small geological museum on the way to it), Cape Chèvre cliffs are 700 million years old and are covered by a rare and beautiful heath based on Bell heather, ling, and Le Gall gorse. The walk around the cape is rather disappointing, the views being generally foreshortened by the bracken (which also houses many biting insects) only being open at the cape itself - and nowhere are they as impressive as at Penhir Point (see below).

18.5   Camaret - A Mini Stonehenge

Tourist Office: 15, Quai Kleber, 29570. Excellent free maps of the peninsula, town, and of Finistère. Also a handy French/English leaflet on the town.

> **Open:** July - Aug, daily, 9am to 7pm, except Sunday - 10am to 1pm.
> Rest of year, 9am to noon, 2pm to 7pm.
> **Website:** www.camaret-sur-mer.com
> **Email:** ot.camaret@wanadoo.fr

Camaret is a lovely sheltered port, at the very tip of the peninsula. There are plenty of shops and restaurants here, and a remarkable **stone circle** - a 'mini-stonehenge' - that lies on the road out to the Pen Hir point. It has forty-one standing quartz stones, which outline a rectangular space 600 yards in length at its base. In Britain it would have fences, wires, a toll booth, interpretation centre - and a staff trained to take money. The **Lagatjar menhirs** stand on a green, virtually disregarded, giving the discoverer a real thrill of pleasure.

Camaret. Photo, A. Bobrovich, CRTB

Also at Camaret is **the Chateau de Vauban** (as Vauban, a military architect, was such a key figure in French history, I have written a mini-biography about him elsewhere in this book). This fort stands at the end of the long jetty that runs back parallel to the main town waterfront. Walled, moated, and accessible via a little gatehouse reached by means of a drawbridge, it was built in 1689 to guard the approaches to Brest.

Note that the top of the steeple on the church has been truncated - by a canon ball fired from an English man o'war, a fine bit of marksmanship if it was really the target. There are three **beaches** here, one is the town beach, another to the west **(no bathing allowed here)** and one to the south (near the parking for the Pen Hir headland). In summer Penn Ar Bed (www.penn-ar-bed.fr) operates a **ferry** service from Camaret to the islands of Ouessant and Sein, while Finist'Mer sails to Ouessant only. There are also cruises out to Pen Hir head.

A Little History

Camaret, or Kameled, was the principal storm port of Finistère. Its sheltered cove harboured ships that could not navigate the Brest Strait in rough seas. In May 1801, the American engineer Robert Fulton, who had studied in England, offered to build a submarine for the French emperor, Napoleon Bonaparte: 'Considering the great importance of diminishing the Power of the British Fleets, I have Contemplated the Construction of a Mechanical Nautulus... the destruction of the English Navy will ensure the independence of the seas and France, the Nation which has most natural resources and population, will alone and without a rival hold the balance of power in Europe.' It is just possible that Fulton's bid was more mercenary than conscientious, as he was at pains to stipulate: 'That the Government of France Contract to pay the Nautulus Company £400 per Gun for each British Ship over 40 tons which they may destroy... that the sum be paid in cash." The submarine was to be rowed by four men. It was tested off Camaret. Fulton's experiments failed and this fine fellow eventually went to work for a higher bidder - the British! Fulton eventually found fame in putting into service the world's first steam ship. In a later war, submarines operating from Brittany (Brest, Lorient and St Nazaire), albeit of German rather than American design, were to bring Britain to the brink of defeat. Camaret's fleet, which once sailed far-off seas, is largely gone now. Perhaps in memory of it, a few derelict wooden boats have been picturesquely left along the foreshore.

18.6 Pen Hir Point / The Beach

Passing the stone circle (see above), the road to Pen Hir point passes some magnificent second world war bunkers, one of which houses a small museum of the Atlantic war (open summer months 10am to noon, 2pm to 6pm). On your left, there is a small road going down toward a fine beach called Veryac'h.

Photo: A. Bobrovich, CRTB

Straight ahead is the parking for the Pen Hir headland. The short walk onto the headland takes you along high, white cliffs of armorican sandstone, which extend into the sea to the Tas de Pois (heap of peas), steep islets detached from the coast. This inaccessible ornithological sanctuary shelters nesting seabirds. On your walk (weather permitting!) you will have the most magnificent views of bays, cliffs and beaches.

18.7 Pointe des Espagnols (Spanish point)

Go back through Camaret and up a road which passes through old and ruined fortifications (the headland was a military preserve at one time). In 1594 after the defeat of their armada which attempted to invade England, the Spanish built a fort here, to blockade Brest. They were driven out after a bitter battle by a combined Anglo-French force. From this 200 foot cliff, there is an exceptional panorama over Brest and its estuary. The area is squeezed into a gorse and blackthorn heath, which is invading the military remains. This point differs from Pen Hir point in that there are no long walks here: but there is often a trailer parked in the carpark, selling food and drink. Here also are later blockhouses, right up to those of the second world war, showing the high strategic importance of this point, dominating the roadstead of Brest, one of France's chief ports.

19. Brest

The Naval Fortress

Brest. Population 150,000

Brest is not the prettiest town in the world. It was bombed almost to destruction in the second world war, when it was home to a large part of Hitler's U-boat submarine fleet. Rebuilt in the 1950s and 60s in the universal house style of concrete ugly, it is rarely attractive. It is, however, set in a very fine natural harbour, and this, as well as its resulting maritime importance, makes it a very interesting place, for adults and children alike.

19.1 Océanopolis

Photo: Y. Gladu, CRTB

The Océanopolis sea life centre is very popular, so it is best to start here, both to avoid the queues and to allow yourself time to enjoy it properly. The centre is located to the east of, and just outside, Brest. It is a massive complex, housing its 42 tanks in 3 pavilions, with 1000 different species on display. Oceanopolis is an amazing and humbling experience of the world's diversity of marine life. Each of the three pavilions covers a maritime zone, polar, temperate and tropical. **The polar pavilion** has three species of penguins and a real ice shelf, seals and penguins can be watched both above and below the water. Then there is feeding time.

The Temperate Pavilion covers the Breton coast, with a film and a touch pool.

The Tropical Pavilion has tanks representing different tropical seas, with sharks, multi-coloured fish, a 13 metre long coral reef, even a bit of tropical jungle.

In summer all three areas are included in one ticket, but in winter you can choose to visit just one or two of them, paying a smaller price. It is a hands-on experience and with a strong focus on education as it is a leading research centre for the study of the world's oceans. You can take a picnic, buy sandwiches there or eat at the self-service café or restaurant at Océanopolis. Free access to the shops and restaurants.

Open: 2nd week in April to 1st week in September, daily 9am to 6pm. Rest of the year, 10am to 5pm, closed Mondays except during French school holidays.
Cost: Adult – 15.40€. Age 4 to 17 & students - 10.80€. Under 4 - free.
Large families (2 adults + 3 children) - 58.00€ + 10% per additional child.
Website: www.oceanopolis.com – with English version

19.2 The Town of Brest

There is a fine group of attractions in the town within easy walking distance of each other. If necessary, all can be driven to.

The best place to start is the **Tourist Office** in the Place de la Liberté, 29200, near the Hotel de Ville, (parking close by), as they give out excellent free maps of the town.

Open: July and Aug, Mon to Sat, 9.30am to 7pm, Sun & bank holidays,10am to noon. Rest of year, Mon to Sat, 9.30am to 6pm, closed Sunday and bank holidays.
Website: www.brest-metropole-tourisme.fr - no English version at time of writing.
Email: office.de.tourisme.brest@wanadoo.fr

Brest and Océanopolis

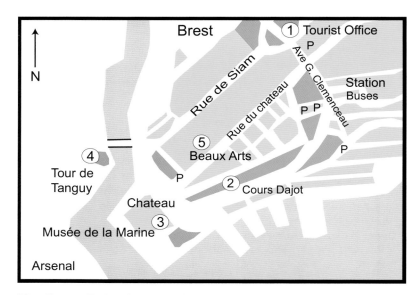

The **Cours Dajot** (named after a director of fortifications) is a fine 600 metre promenade to the east of the chateau. From it there is a splendid panoramic view of the deep water harbour of Brest.

Le Musée de la Marine. Housed in the Chateau de Brest, an impressive medieval castle, the naval museum has a fine collection of model ships, paintings and sculptures.
   Open: April until mid September, 10am to 6.30pm.
   Cost: Adult - 5.00€. Under 18 - free.

The Tour de Tanguy Museum. Wall paintings showing Brest as it was before the bombing. Also, great views.
   Open: 10am to noon, 2pm to 6pm in season.
   Cost: Free.

The Arsenal can also be visited by EEC nationals between mid June and mid September. A passport is needed. Ask at the tourist office.

Musée des Beaux Arts. 17th to 20th century Italian, Flemish and French painters. Painters of the Pont Aven (Breton) school.
Open: 10am to noon, 2pm to 6pm, closed Tues, Sun mornings and bank holidays.
Cost: Adults - 4€. Under 18 - free.

A Little History

Brest began as a Roman settlement and was the centre of a kingdom after the collapse of the Roman empire. The city was heavily involved, as was all of Brittany, in the struggle between the English (initially Anglo-Normans, i.e. Normans who had conquered England) and France, for the possession of the land.
The young duke, Arthur of Brittany, was hidden in the castle here from Richard the Lionheart (not at all the nice chap as portrayed by Disney), who wished to overthrow him. The town around the base of the castle was walled in the fourteenth century. Brest was occupied by the English in 1342. Besieged by the Breton dukes at the head of 10,000 men, the English finally evacuated the fortress in 1397. In 1532, Brittany was swallowed up by France and Brest was fortified anew by, among others, the ubiquitous Vauban (see the section on Vauban). In the 17th century, Cardinal Richelieu had the first naval arsenal constructed to give a major naval base on the Atlantic seaboard. This was completed 50 years later. In 1685 a Jesuit College was founded here, to furnish priests for His Majesty's navy. Brest grew considerably in the eighteenth and nineteenth centuries. The French naval college and a training school for young seamen were established here, in two ships in the harbour. For many years, therefore, Brest was the principal port of the French navy: and they are still there in strength.

Brest and Océanopolis

Brest was, as has been noted, a main port for the German submarine fleet which nearly brought Britain to starvation in the second world war. The submarine pens were repeatedly bombed, but never destroyed. The town, on the other hand, was.

The bay of Brest has a circumference of about 40 km (25 miles) and its only entry from the sea is le Goulet (the gullet), which is dominated by fortifications.

Tonnerre de Brest (Brest thunder), Captain Haddock's preferred curse in the Tintin stories, refers to the cannon which was fired to signal the escape of a prisoner from the Brest fortress.

Brest castle. Photo, J-P. Gratien, CRTB

20. Ile d'Ouessant

Lighthouses and the Sleepless Sea

Population 900.

Known in English as Ushant, the Île d'Ouessant lies to the west of Brest and forms part of the Armorique nature reserve. The island is 7km - 4 miles long and 4km - 2.5 miles wide. It is a plateau, peaking at over 60 m (nearly 200 feet). There are important colonies of sea birds, especially in autumn during migration. Seals and dolphins can sometimes be seen offshore (indeed there is a dolphin tour boat from Le Conquet, see next day out).

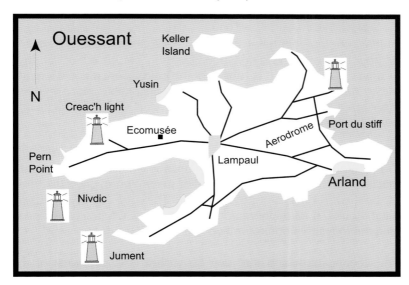

The ferry docks at the modern harbour in the ominous-sounding Baie du Stiff. There's a scattering of houses here, and more dotted around the island, but the single town – with the only hotels, restaurants and shops – is 3km away at Lampaul.

Ile d'Ouessant

There are bicycles to hire at the harbour, evidently a thriving concern as there are 4 different hirers, each with probably a hundred bikes. Hiring a bike is a good idea, as the island is a bit too big (the coastline is 28 kilometres) to explore on foot. The path around the island is not to be cycled on, so one needs to visit a headland, cycle back a little inland and then cycle to the next (a map is provided by the bike hire people).

The bikes cost around 15 euros per day for a V.T.T – mountain bike. The island is a delight to cycle round, there being very few cars. It is quite hilly, which means short sharp pedalling up to the headlands: but then you are infinitely rewarded by the superb sea views from the cliff tops. The cycling is across open heath, down tracks that sometimes merit the all terrain cycles (they work well).

At least once a year gales in excess of 200 km (about 125 miles) an hour howl over the island, and Ouesaant can be cut off for days at a time. Otherwise, it is really not the cold, scary place it's made out to be. On the contrary, it's quite a hospitable place and, as mentioned, excellent for a bike ride, weaving along the tracks and headlands between Stiff Bay and Pern Point.

The nearest headland to the dock houses '1' lighthouse, called Stiff. The counting of lighthouses on Ouessant is difficult. The island's officially has four, of France's total of thirty. You might think three of them were on this headland alone. They are, strictly speaking a lighthouse, a semaphore and a radar tower. On this headland is also the inevitable bunker or two, left by the Germans.

The second headland that can be visited is to the west of the bay of Beninou, giving wonderful views over the island of Keller. The plage of Yusin is sandy but not terribly inspiring. The better beaches being south of Lampaul and Porz Arland (near where the ferry comes in), where there is a small harbour and a delightful sheltered beach for safe swimming.

Lampaul is the island's only town. There is a **Tourist Office** here.
Open: July and Aug, Mon to Sat, 10am to noon, 1.30pm to 5pm,
Sunday 10am to noon.

Lampaul. Photo, J.P. Gratien, CRTB

At the church in Lampaul is a chapel containing wax proëlla crosses symbolising the many islanders who never returned from the sea. The ceremony was unique in the Christian world. A small cross of sanctified wax, hardly larger than a hand, represented the dead sailor. This would be watched over in his house overnight, then taken in procession to the church where it would be given a burial ceremony and eventually placed in the chapel. The last ceremony took place in 1962. In the graveyard are the graves of 3 Allied serviceman from the First World War.

The Phare (light house) du Créac'h, is a tall white tower with black bands, housing the most powerful light in Europe (61 km visibility). It stands at an eerie and wild spot, with monstrous seas crashing against the rocks even on the calmest days. There are strange rocks that sometimes seem to have a human appearance, and odd structures high and inaccessible on the cliffs (one was once the housing for swinging an underwater bell, to warn shipping!).

In the old machine room of the light house is situated the French National Lighthouse Museum.

Open: Mid July to Aug, daily, 10.30am to 6.30pm, 9pm to 11pm. April, Tue to Sun, 2pm to 6.30pm. May to mid July & Sept, daily 10.30am to 6.30pm. Oct to March, Tue to Sun, 2pm to 4pm.
Cost: Adult - 6.50€. Child (8 to 14) - 4,10€. Under 7 – free. The ticket is also valid for the ecomuseum, see below. A ticket for only one or other attraction costs 4.10€ for an adult, 2.60€ for a child

The Ecomuseum of Niou Huella is actually two houses, one of which is a museum of island history and the other a reconstruction of a traditional island house, complete with two massive "box beds", one for the parents and the other for the children. The furnishings in the houses of Ouessant always included a box bed, bench and table, painted (with the remains of paint from the boats) to disguise the different woods used, sometimes the remains of ship wrecks. It forms half of the Eco-Musée d'Ouessant, in combination with the Creac'h lighthouse (see above) Same opening hours and prices as the museum (see above).

Ouessant. Photo, G. Fisher, CRTB

A Little History

Ouessant has always been a major point on the shipping lane up the coast of Europe. In the 4th century B.C. the Greek Pytheas reported the Celtic name for Ouessant, Uxisama.

This, mist shrouded island, like Anglesey, was a holy island of the Druids. Almost 3,000 people used to live on the island. In general, the women farmed while the men folk fished - at any one time, only a quarter of the inhabitants were men, the others being at sea. And the sea took them. Between 1746 and 1784, for example, 230 men from the island – from a total island population of about 1600 - perished at sea. The women tilled the land. There being little wood on the island, the fires were fed by heather roots, turf, sea weed and dried cow dung. On the eternal fire, a stockpot would be set at morning to heat the evening meal. Wood was not to be wasted, and driftwood and wreckage was put to use in furnishing the houses. Each house was a miniature farm, with common pasturing rights across the island. The locals raised sheep and lamb in the salty fields: ragoût de mouton (lamb baked under a layer of roots and herbs) remains a staple dish.

Dozens of small windmills once dotted the island (only one survives). While the inhabitants are no longer isolated from the rest of the world, centuries of tradition prevail: houses are painted blue and white for the Virgin Mary, or green and white to symbolise hope.
The local saying 'He who sees Ouessant sees his blood' arises from the fact that, in the old days, by the time that sailors spotted the island looming up through the fog, it was often already too late to take avoiding action. Before the construction of the lighthouses there were six or seven major shipwrecks a year on the island, mostly occurring on the 50 days each year when visibility is less than a thousand yards. Today, these lighthouses guard the busiest sea lane in the world. A quarter of the earth's shipping trade goes past the island, up to 500 merchant ships a day.

How to get there
Note: if you're just going for the day, it's a good idea to buy a picnic before you set out – the Lampaul shops have limited and rather pricey supplies.

Two ferry companies serve the islands, a fast one (Vedettes rapides) and a slower one (Penn ar bed). The prices are very similar. **Both companies advise that you book 2 days ahead in high season, so it is worth planning the trip ahead.**

The ferry company **Finist'mer**. Plus points. Fast boats. Minus points, can only buy tickets from their ports (not in tourist information offices).
> **Website:** www.finist-mer.fr - in French only.

The ferry company **Penn ar Bed**. Plus points. Tickets available from 40 tourist offices in Finistère (ask at any tourist office for a list).
> **Website:** www.pennarbed.com - in French only.

The departure times and prices given here were correct at time of printing, but it is worth checking the websites or in local tourist offices to see whether they have changed.

Cost
Prices shown are for adults and are approximate (for example, in high season there is a surcharge of 1 to 2 euros per person). Children's (age 3 – 16) prices are roughly 60% of adults. Under 4's are 1 euro each.

The Four Routes

1. Le Conquet – Ouessant (Adult return approximately 27€)
Penn ar Bed 75 minute crossing - stops at Molene on the way. All year round. Up to 3 sailings a day in the season (from 8.30am onwards). Finist'mer. 35 minute crossing. From early April until end September. 3 to 5 sailings a day. Check for times.

2. Camaret - Ouessant (Adult return approximately 28€)
Finist'mer 1 hour crossing. 1st week in May to mid June - Thursday only. Mid June to mid Sept. Daily service, either at 8.45am or 9.30am. Free parking at Camaret.
Penn ar Bed About 2 hour crossing (may stop at Molene on the way). 8th July to 27th Aug, Mon to Sat, 8.40am. 26th April to 7th Jul & 28th Aug to 15th Sep, Wednesdays 8.40am.

3. Landilut - Ouessant (Adult return approx 28€)
Finist'mer 30 minute crossing. Parking free at Landilut. 4th July to 28th August, up to 3 services a day. Check with tourist office for times.

4. Brest - Ouessant (Adult return approx 31€)
Finist'mer An hour and a quarter crossing. Check with tourist office for times and dates.
Penn ar Bed Two and a half hour crossing (stops on the way at Le Conquet and sometimes Molene). Every day of the year at 8.30am (enquire with company for return times).

Or you could fly...

In addition, you can fly to Ouessant with Finist'Air. The fifteen minute flight leaves Brest's Guipavas airport daily at 8.30am and 4.45pm (correct at time of printing, but check these times).
Cost: Fares are one way. For return fares, double the price. Adult - 63€. Aged 2 to 12 - 36€. Groups of three or more adults go for 52€ each, each way. For fares for a trip of 3 or more days, see the website.
Website: www.finistair.fr. - in French and English.

Le Conquet and Area

21. Around le Conquet

A Coastal Day out with Excellent Views

21.1 Le Conquet – Beaches and Dolphins

Population 2400. The Market is on Tuesday morning.

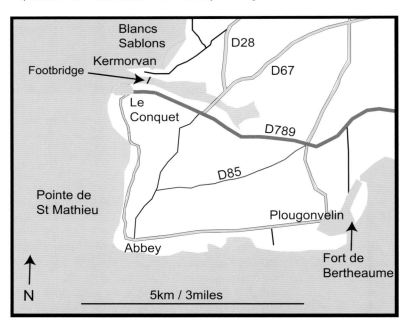

The **Tourist Office**, Parc de Beauséjour, 29217, give a useful map of the town, as well as information about the boat trips which can be had from here (dolphin watching as well as to the islands. For details about sailings to Ouessant, see the entry for the island).
   Open: In season 10am to noon, 2pm to 6pm.
   Website: www.leconquet.fr (Only 1st page has an English translation).
   Email: tourisme@leconquet.fr

The town and its environs are well worth a visit, being pretty much unspoilt. It's very much a working fishing village, with grey-stone houses leading down to the stone jetties of a cramped harbour: a little odd in that the shops and restaurants are a couple of hundred yards from the sea, while at the sea itself there are none. The town has some high quality sea food restaurants and the seaweed cake at the boulangerie is rather fine too (if there's any left). The town has a small sandy beach and others on the other side of the river. Go across the footbridge (passerelle de Croaie) to the presqu'ile (peninsula) of **Kermorvan**, a headland of about a mile long where a footpath leads up to the point. The point has the customary second world war pillbox or two and a lighthouse (not open to the public). The estuary is a fine place for bird watching - egrets being plentiful. On returning on the northern coast of the peninsula, there is a fine golden sand beach which slopes gently into the sea. Further along is the wind-surfing beach of **les Blancs Sablons**, which stretches for a couple of miles.

21.2 Boat trips to see the Dolphins

There is a company (Vedette Aquafaune) here who do trips around the bay in a glass bottomed boat. This is partly to see the fields of seaweed which are harvested here (and the fish, the sea is extremely clear), partly to see a small colony of seals, mostly to see the dolphins. The trips last about two and a half hours. There is a commentary, but it is in French only: and to the average English speaking visitor it is largely incomprehensible.

However, if the dolphins are seen, then it is all worth while, as they are spectacular, exploding out of the water round the boat. The dolphins turn up for 90% of the trips (they did on ours). We saw a pod of 20 to 30 dolphins who leaped out of the water two or three together, synchronised. Pure performers, they went ahead, came back and generally played to the audience. A joy.

Boat times are governed by the tides, so ask at the tourist office, or the harbour. It is highly advised that you book ahead, especially in the summer months, or you may not get on.

> **Cost:** Adult - 25€. Age 4 to 16 - 15€. Under 4 - 2€.

21.3 Abbey above the Waves

The nearby headland of **Pointe St Mathieu** is a beautiful one, with free parking, a ruined abbey (bashed about by the Vikings but in use until the revolution), a lighthouse, a signalling station and grassy cliff top walks with wonderful views across the sea.

Pointe St Mathieu Photo: G. Fisher, CRTB

The cliffs are ideal for a picnic, assuming it's not foggy or blowing a gale. The volume of shipping that passes by within sight of land here is staggering, so when it isn't foggy, you can sit there with binoculars watching ships go by all day. There is also a small museum here.

> **Open:** daily, July and August 10.30am to 12.30pm, 2pm to 7pm.
> **Cost:** not available at time of printing, but probably minimal.

Across the road is a gift shop and a hotel/restaurant (menus from 25€ to 65€). The hotel's website, www.pointe-saint-mathieu.com has some good photos. From April to October, you can climb to the top of **the lighthouse,** 56m high, for a guided visit. Splendid seascapes with many islands and islets far below.

Open times: (approximately). Mid July to 3rd week Aug, daily, 10am to 7.30pm. Rest of July and August, 10am to noon, 2pm to 7pm. End of March to June and Sept and Oct, weekends, 3pm to 6pm.
Cost: Adult - 2€. Age 6-11 - 1€. Under 6 - free.

The Abbey, which is small and free to wander around, once possessed the head of Saint Mathew... the story goes back to the 6th century, when Breton traders in Ethiopia 'found' the bones of the saint. After many weeks at sea, as they approached this point, a violent storm blew up. Terrified, the sailors called on Saint Mathew to save them. The headland reputedly drew apart, allowing the sailors to safely land at le Conquet. The grateful sailors placed St Mathew's skull on the headland that now bears his name and a monastery grew up around it, which then became the abbey.

21.4 Bertheaume - An Island Fort

The island fort is one of the oldest parts of the defence works of the Brest channel. Vauban (who else, see entry on Vauban) first put cannons there, which proved effective against the failed English landing at Camaret in 1694. Fully restored, it is well worth a visit (underground gunpowder room, battlements).

Open: July - Aug, daily, 10am to 7pm. June and Sept
Weekends and bank holidays 2pm to 6pm.
Cost: Adult - 2.50€. Age 6 to 11 -1.50€. Under 6 - free. There is a creperie nearby.

22. North Finistére

Land of Churches and Wolves

This route contains several possible attractions. To do all of them in one day would probably be too much. I present them here so that you can pick and mix according to your tastes and circumstances.

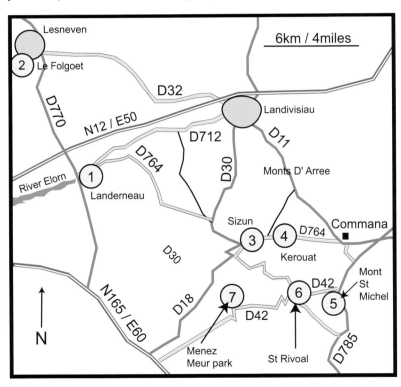

I start the route at Landerneau, about 5 miles east of Brest, but, of course, you can start it wherever is most convenient for you.

Two of the 'stops' on this circuit – at Le Folgoët and Sizun - are at Parish Closes. There are three circuits of parish closes in the area (further information from the tourist offices). If you are interested in church architecture and customs in Brittany please read the section 'Religious Brittany'.

22.1 Landerneau

Markets on Tuesday morning, Friday morning and all day Saturday.

Salmon and trout are fished for from this interesting old port. There are many restaurants here. The **Tourist office**, pont de Rohan, 29800, is as its address suggests, on the bridge. The bridge house used to be a prison, but the prisoners had the habit of pulling up the floorboards and jumping into the river. Here can be had an interesting brochure, in interesting English, and a map of a town trail showing some fine buildings.

Open: July & Aug, Mon to Sat, 9.15am to 12.30pm, 1.30pm to 7pm, Sunday, 10am to 1pm. Rest of year, Tue to Sat, 9am to noon, 2pm to 6pm (5pm out of season).
Website: www.tourisme-landerneau-daoulas.fr - French and Breton only.
Email: ot.payslanderneau-daoulas@wanadoo.fr

Landerneau, photo R. Tanguy, CRTB

22.2 Le Folgoët (Lesneven)

The joined towns of Le Folgoët and Lesneven make for quite a large town. Le Folgoët, which is on the southern edge, is noted for its religious festival, the Pardon (see the section 'Religious Brittany') which takes place on the 1st Sunday in July and the previous Friday and Saturday. The wide approach to the church is too small to hold the crowds on pardon days – the pardon here being one of the biggest in Brittany.

The church of **Notre Dame** is in the Gothic style. It was built in the fifteenth century and is notable for its carvings, its many gilded life-size statues and its two spires, particularly the fine North Tower, which is 54 metres (170 feet) high. It was built on a Druidic holy spring (many chapels and churches in Brittany are built on Druid holy springs). Pilgrims come to drink from the fountain, which is outside the church.

Glass at le Folgoet: M. S-Kellinghaus, CRTB

There is a small **Folk Museum** opposite which deals with the region from its earliest history, and also has costumes and furnishings, as well as a collection of religious art.

> **Open:** In summer, Wed to Mon, 2pm to 6pm.
> **Cost:** Adult - 2.50€. Child (12-18) - 1€. Under 12 – free.

22.3 Sizun - A Fine Parish Close

A very fine example of a **Parish Close** (see religious Brittany) in a pleasant little village. The three monumental arches are the pride of this village, making one of the the largest and most spectacular of the Breton closes. The old ossuary (where the bones were kept when the graveyard was cleared out for new burials) houses a small free museum, where can be seen a Breton box bed and some costumes. There is a creperie and a couple of restaurants here.

22.4 The Mills of Kerouat

Part of the group of Breton ecomuseums, which show country life in the past, The Moulins de Kerouat are a group of some 15 buildings erected between the 15th and 20th centuries. The houses, mills, bread ovens, springs, washing pool and lake are spread over 30 acres. The interior of one house has period Breton furniture, such as tables and box beds. The explanations on the exhibits are only in French, but one is given a leaflet in English which explains each building in brief, and the exhibits, being fairly low tech, are not difficult to follow. A small but powerfully evocative museum which is well worth an hour or two. No restaurant or café.

> **Open:** (ticket office) June, Mon to Fri, 10am to 6pm, Sat & Sun, 2pm to 6pm. July and Aug, every day, 11am to 7pm. Mid April, May, Sept and Oct, Mon to Fri, 10am to 6pm, Sat, Sun & Bank holidays, 2pm to 6pm. The ticket office closes 1 hour before the museum.
> **Cost:** Adult - 4.50€. Child (8 to 14) - 2.10€. Under 8 - free.

22.5 View point on St Michel Mountain

Follow the signposted route from the D785, park, then climb the hill with the chapel on top. This windy eminence with its unfurnished chapel is very atmospheric and gives great views over the Arrée and Black Mountains. At 380 metres (1246ft) this is one of the highest points in Brittany and gives, unusually, a real moorland scene with rocky outcrops and peat bogs, as well as rivers and lakes.

22.6 Maison Cornec - A Peasant's Lot

At St Rivoal, the Maison Cornec is another example of the sensitivity of the Bretons in preserving interesting buildings (the ecomuseum concept). The farmhouse, with its outside staircase, dates from 1702 and is sited in a wooded valley. Farmer and animals lived under the same roof. The living room, with its floor of beaten earth and its furnishings visible in the dim light from small windows, brings to life the living conditions of a 17th century peasant.

> **Open:** July and August, daily, 11am to 7pm. June, daily, 2pm to 6pm. 1st august to 15th September, daily, except Saturday, 2pm to 6pm. The ticket office closes half an hour before the museum.
> **Cost:** 1€

22.7 Menez Meur Wildlife Park

This 520 hectare park in the heart of the Monts d'Arrée is a tribute to Brittany's natural heritage, sheltering and protecting flora, wildlife and remarkable landscapes. Three trails - animals (wolves, cows, pigs, etc, 3.3km), forests (2.5km) and landscapes (8.5km) - are open to the public for exploring the park with or without a guide. Picnic area and children's games. Food available between June and September.

> **Open:** July and August, daily, 10am to 7pm. June and Sept, daily, 10am to 6pm. Mar, Apr, May, Oct, Nov, Wed & Sun, 1pm to 5.30pm.
> Cost: Adult - 3.30€. Age 8 to 14 - 2.10€. Under 8 - free.
> **Website:** www.parc-naturel-armorique.fr (covers the whole of the national park in which Menez Meur is situated. In French only)
> **Email:** domaine.menez.meur@pnr-armorique.fr

23. Roscoff and Batz

Town of Granite, Island of Flowers

23.1 Roscoff

Population 3800. Market, Wednesday mornings.

Roscoff is well known for its temperate climate (influenced by the Gulf Stream), its beautiful coastline and its marine cures. It is a granite town, like much of Brittany. The stone, its dignified architecture and its sea-faring people have all moulded its character. It is a very interesting place with lots to see and do.

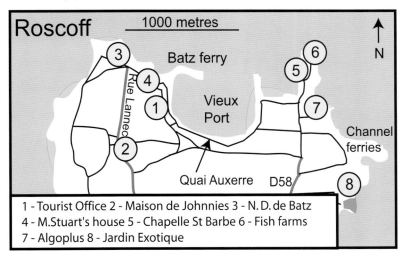

Roscoff

1000 metres

Batz ferry

Vieux Port

Channel ferries

Quai Auxerre   D58

1 - Tourist Office 2 - Maison de Johnnies 3 - N. D. de Batz
4 - M.Stuart's house 5 - Chapelle St Barbe 6 - Fish farms
7 - Algoplus 8 - Jardin Exotique

The **Tourist Office**, 46, rue Gambetta, 29680, gives brochures on the attractions mentioned below and one or two others. Useful maps.
Open: July and August, Mon to Sat, 9am to 12.30pm, 1.30pm to 7pm, Sunday and public holidays, 10am to 12.30pm, 2pm to 5pm. Rest of year, Mon to Sat, 9am to noon, 2pm to 6pm.
Website: www.roscoff-tourisme.com (has English translation)
Email: tourisme.roscoff@wanadoo.fr

Roscoff and Batz

The granite town, bedecked with flowers, has interesting small streets, especially in the old town (behind the Vieux Port). Here can be seen the often richly sculpted facades of the houses of merchants and corsairs, dating from the 16th and 17th centuries. The oldest buildings are in the Gothic style, either in finished or undressed stone. With towers, spiral stairs, great chimney stacks, gargoyles and windows poking forward from the roof line, this is a true rubber-necking area. Some of the houses have cellar entrances straight onto the beach.

Roscoff. Photo: CRTB

Maison des Johnnies

The French onion seller on his bike used to be a common sight in Britain. Roscoff is where they came from. In 1828, one Henri Olivier filled a sack with onions and began the trade. He was followed by hundreds of others called 'Johnny Onions', so that by 1929 there were 1500 of them.

They would carry as much as 100kg on their bikes and travelled as far afield as Scotland (as evidenced by their common appearance in the Beano and Dandy comics whose home is Dundee). You could say that Brittany Ferries is the lineal descendant of this tradition (see below). This museum celebrates the tradition.

Open: July and Aug, 3pm to 7pm, except Sat (rest of year, on pre-booking only).
Cost: Adult - 4€. Age 10 to 18 - 2.50€. Under 10 - free.

Notre Dame de Croatz Batz is a 16th century church with a wonderful lantern belfry, one of the finest in Finistère. The outside walls and tower have sculptures of ships and cannons.

Marie Stuart's house The chapel that Mary Stuart (see below) prayed at was demolished in 1932 and the door and font were incorporated in this house.

From **La Chapelle Sainte Barbe**, a fine view extends over the town and port. Below the chapel are **Fish farms** (viviers). There are walkways between pools containing salmon, trout, lobster, spiny lobster and crab.

Algoplus, zone du Blascon. This is something different. A guided tour, free, in French, of a seaweed processing factory. With tastings and recipes.

Open: July and August, daily at 11am, 3pm, 4pm and 5pm.
April to June, 11am & 3pm. Sept - Nov, 3pm.

Jardin Exotique. 3 hectares (7 acres) of tropical gardens. A sub-tropical paradise at the foot of the Roch Hiévec which dominates Roscoff. 3000 varieties of tropical plants. With turtles in the ponds and cacti in the rocks, prepare to be entranced.

Open: 1st June to 30th September, daily, 10am to 7pm. Rest of year, daily but closes between 12.30pm and 2pm. Closed Dec - Feb.
Cost: Adult - 5.00€. Age 12 to 18 - 2.50€. Under 12 - free.

A Little History

Roscoff began as a small fishing village. The current town was begun around 1400 and grew with maritime trade. When trade faltered due to wars, the Roscoffians became pirates in the service of the king, and smugglers. Of course, much of the trade, as well as many of the fights, were with England.

Mary Queen of Scots landed here in 1548 (aged 6!) on her way to Paris to be engaged to François, the son and heir of Henri II. Bonnie Prince Charlie arrived here in 1746, after his defeat at Culloden. The motto of the town is 'Hit hard, hit heavy, hit always.'

Brittany Ferries - Worthy Heir to a Fine Tradition

It is obvious to any visitor to Brittany that the lifeblood of the place is the sea. As the **Histoire de la Bretagne** so poetically puts it: "Figurehead of the great vessel of Europe, she thrusts foursquare into the ocean, which savages and tears at her flanks, panting ozone and mist over her lands."

Somewhere in the background of all of the great Breton folk tales - and what a wealth of them there are, whether it be Tristan and Isolde, the island of Ys, or the Authurian cycle – is the sea. Down the centuries, the bulk of the French navy has been Breton. Tintin's companion, the fierce black-bearded Captain Haddock, is, of course, a Breton whose favourite oath is Tonnerre de Brest (referring to the cannon which was fired in Brest to signal an escape from the fortress).

Jacques Cartier, discoverer of Canada, was a St Malo man – and the Falkland Islands owe their French and Spanish names (Malouines/Malvinas) to his home town.
Then there are the sailors of the Island of Sein who sailed en masse to Britain in 1940, and the Bretons who travelled to Britain each year to sell onions…. and their lineal descendants who now provide the great bulk of ferries between Brittany and Britain….

Brittany Ferries, whose home port is Roscoff, is in many ways the antithesis of what the British think of as typical French companies, i.e. state owned monopolies who compete unfairly.

The company was started in 1973 by the Breton Co-operative, headed by Alexis Gourvennec, to get vegetables from Petite Bretagne to Grande Bretagne. Gourvennec, who left school at 16, was then 37 years old. Today the enterprise employs 3,000 people, provides a quarter of the French merchant navy, and serves the best food I've tasted on the Channel. That the company is Breton goes without saying. Brittany Ferries is a credit to Breton industry, and a worthy heir to its homeland's maritime tradition.

Batz. Photo, H. Marcou, CRTB

23.2   L'ile de Batz

Permanent population – 800. Post code 29253.

The island of Batz lies 2 kilometres from Roscoff. The island is 3.5 kilometres long (about 2 miles) by 1.5km wide. It has a small village with several shops and eating places and many sandy beaches on the east coast.

With its own micro-climate (in advance of the mainland), the island has a very rich flora and fauna. The island lives from tourism, fishing and farming. The north of the island is farmed intensively, seaweed being used to compost the fields. There are 13 kilometres of tracks, and bikes can be hired on the island.

There is an **exotic garden** on Batz, with 1500 species from countries such as south Africa and Chile. The garden is built on the site of a village, swallowed up by sand. Sheltered from the winds, it is a wonderful place.

Open: July and August, daily, 1pm to 6pm. April to June & Sept to Oct, daily, except Tuesday, 2pm to 6pm.

Cost: Adult - 4.50€. Child (10 to 16) - 2.50€. Under 10 - free.

To the west of the island, towards Toull ar Sarpant, where the sea rolls in a strange manner, legend tells that in the fifth century Paul-Aurélien (a Celtic saint from Britain) cast out a terrible serpent from the island.

The Lighthouse (Le Phare)

Open: July and August, daily 1pm to 5.30pm. June and first 2 weeks in September, daily except Wednesday, 2pm to 5pm.

Cost: Adult - 2.0€. Child (6 -12) - 1€. Under 6 – free.

How to get there

The crossings are from the old harbour (vieux port) in Roscoff every 30 minutes in summer and take a quarter of an hour. Reservations are not necessary.

Cost (return): Adult - 7.00€. Age 4 to 11 - 4.00€. Bikes: 7€.

24. Morlaix and Wild Places

Of Beer, Wolves and Wild Places

24.1 Morlaix - The Town that Bit Back

Population 16,000. Market, all day Saturday.

Morlaix is set between three hills, which are spanned by a magnificent granite railway viaduct, 292 metres long and 58 metres (180ft) high. This carries the Paris to Brest main line. The town has steep lanes (venelles), sometimes stepped, and paved streets lined with old residences.

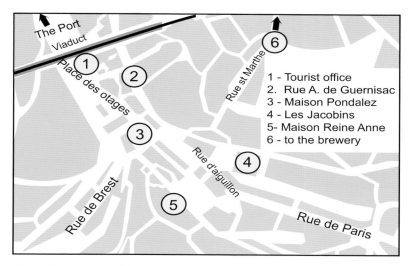

1 - Tourist office
2. Rue A. de Guernisac
3 - Maison Pondalez
4 - Les Jacobins
5- Maison Reine Anne
6 - to the brewery

The oldest type of house are the **Maisons à Lanterne** (Lantern Houses) or, in Breton, **Pondalez**, and they are unique to Morlaix. These three and four storey buildings were built in the 15th and 16th centuries.

Long, rectangular terraced houses, they had their fronts to the street and their backs to the town wall, so they had little light. To overcome this, the central halls were left open to the roof and lit from above, with skylights. These halls typically house a massive ornate fireplace and are served by a spiral staircase, from which wooden passages sprout off at each floor level. The town still has a dozen of them. Morlaix has a pretty port, right in the centre of town. In the summer there is a highly colourful "Art in the Streets" festival, in which street theatre, music and dancing takes place all over the town over five Wednesday evenings from mid July through August.

Photo J.P. Gratien, CRTB

The **Tourist Office**, Place des Otages provides a useful map of the town, with English explanation on one side.
   Open: July and Aug: daily 10am to 7pm, except Sunday and bank hols, when closed 10.30am to 12.30pm. Rest of year: 10am to noon, 2pm to 6pm. Closed Sunday.
   Website: www.morlaixtourisme.fr and www.morlaix.fr
   Email: officetourisme.morlaix@wanadoo.fr

Walking in Morlaix is a treat and just following your nose along the steep Venelles is worthwhile. **The Rue Ange de Guernisac** contains many fine buildings, shops and eating places.

The museum collections of Morlaix are housed in two remarkable buildings (a hundred yards apart). The main building is **Les Jacobins**, an ex-convent, which houses an important and interesting collection of paintings (with a Courbet and a Monet), and Breton themed exhibitions (amongst them marriage, God, the table). The second part of the museum is the **Maison à Pondalez**, a very fine lantern roofed half-timbered building where exhibits are over four floors (daily life, buildings, architecture and history).

> **Open:** July and August: daily, 10am to noon, 2pm to 6.30pm. October to March and June: 10am to noon, 2pm to 5pm, closed Tuesday and Sunday. April, May and Sept: 10am to noon, 2pm to 6pm, except Sun 2pm to 6pm and closed all day Tue
>
> **Cost:** A single ticket suffices for both sites (single site roughly half price). Adult - 4.10€. Children - 2.20€.

The **Maison de la Reine Anne**, at 33 Rue de Mur, is the finest example of the 'Lantern houses' mentioned above. Duchess Anne is reputed to have stayed there (see history section).

> **Open:** July & Aug Mon - Sat 11am to 6.30pm. Sept: Mon - Sat 11am to 5pm. May & June Mon - Sat 11am to 6pm.
>
> **Cost:** 1.60€

For those with a taste for regional beers, The **Deux Rivières** (Two Rivers) Brewery, 1, place de la Madeleine, can be visited Monday to Friday in July and August at 11am and 2pm. This is where Coreff beer is brewed.

A Little History

Morlaix owes its wealth to its maritime activity of the 13th to 18th century. Midway along the maritime route between southern and northern Europe, it was one of the biggest harbours on the English Channel, for dried fish, cloth, wood, leather, paper and wine. Morlaix was also famous for ship building, and some of the ship builders' art can be seen in the carvings and ornamentation of the old house facades.

In 1522, in retaliation for raiding by Morlaisien corsairs, sixty sail of English ships sacked the town: but the English sailors, as was their wont, had a few drops of the hard stuff afterwards (Coreff?) and ended up being beaten up by the locals. This episode is celebrated on the town crest, a lion facing the English leopard and a pun on the town name: 'If they bite you, bite them back !' (S'ils te mordent, mord-les). Well I guess you had to be there. In 1736 the Tobacco Factory was built on the quay. This imposing building was designed by Blondel, the King's architect, for the East India Company. Before the construction of the viaduct, the harbour went right up to the steps of the town hall. The port declined after the French were thrown out of India, recovering for a moment its importance in 1944 as a port for supplies for Patton's armies.

24.2 Wolf Museum - Le Cloître St. Thégonnec

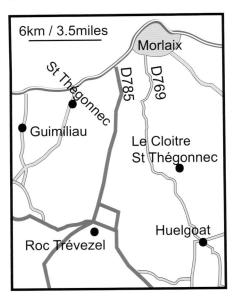

St Thégonnec had wolves until the end of the nineteenth century, so it's appropriate that there is a museum of the wolf here. Nothing in English, but very atmospheric and entertaining for kids as there is a wealth of visual material to look at and some videos of wolves in the wild, etc. It's worth going just for the display of children's drawings and painting of wolves in the entrance corridor which are both hilarious and enchanting.

Open: July and August: daily, 2pm to 6pm (Rest of year: Sunday afternoons only, 2pm to 6pm)
Cost: Adults - 3.50€. Under 14's - 2.50€.

24.3 Huelgoat - In the Steps of Arthur

Huelgoat ("the tall wood") is a small town, bounded on one edge by a lake. It has restaurants, créperies and a supermarket.

The **tourist office** rue du 5 aout 1944 (closed Sunday) has footpath and cycle maps (bikes can be hired in the village by the day, for 10€ for an adult, 7€ for a child). There are guided walks here, in English, led by Wendy Mewes (see section Walking in Brittany). Huelgoat is surrounded by a forest, of about 4 square miles, which has many remarkable natural features. Well marked forest walks lead to gigantic boulders and caves, with rivers and streams flowing between. Two theories are advanced as to the origin of these strange rocks. Geologists say that they were created deep underground from cooling molten rock. Romantics say that they were thrown by the giant Gargantua in response to the poor welcome he got in Huelgoat. In either case, these walks between great granite blocks transport the visitor into a magical world. **Arthur's Cave** (Grotte d'Artus), **Arthur's Camp** (Camp d'Artus, legendry site of King Arthur and the knights of the round table) **the Devils' Cave** (Grotte du Diable), **the Fairy's Lake, the Boars' Lake, the Trembling Rock** (weighs 100 tons). So many mysterious spots, one wouldn't be too surprised to see a group of elves threading its way down a narrow path.

Just one more legend: At the **Gouffre** (the gulf), where the water disappears underground, the water sometimes has a red tinge. This is caused, so it is said, because of the cruelty of Dahut, daughter of Gradlon, king of Ys (see Legendary Brittany). When her boyfriends left her at the break of day, she would give them a mask, supposedly so they could sneak out unrecognised. However, as soon as the unfortunate put it on, it gripped his face and neck and strangled him. A black rider would then gallop with the corpse and dump it here. The spot is still haunted. Approach the gulf at night and you will hear the sobbing of the young men who were thrown there.

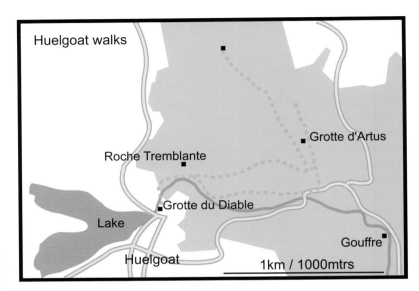

Huelgoat walks

Grotte d'Artus

Roche Tremblante

Grotte du Diable

Lake

Huelgoat

Gouffre

1km / 1000mtrs

24.4 The Poerop Garden and Arboretum

This is a fine 50 acre garden and arboretum, at Huelgoat, with 2,500 species, many of which are rare and endangered plants. With a Medieval garden, apple and nut orchard, bamboo thickets and geographical plantations by area (for example, China, Nepal, South America) as well as rose and aquatic gardens. Tea room.
Open: May until mid Oct, 10am to 6pm - rest of the year closes an hour earlier.
Cost: The garden and arboretum are separate. A visit to one is 5€, both 7€ These charges are for age 12 and over - under 12's are free.

24.5 Trévezel Rock - The High Spot of Brittany

At 384 metres, 1260 ft, the Roc Trévezel is the highest point in Brittany. An open, windy, summit with impressive views. It is a half hour walk (round trip) from the D785 road. Trévezel was the home of a saint. To be granted all that one desired by this good man, all one needed to do was rub his head softly.

But the saint lived inside the mountain. The mountain opened only every 11 years, and to persuade the saint to come out, he had to be asked by a child whose eleventh birthday was that day. An English wizard took such a child to the place on the right day. The child, going into the mountain, found a room full of apples but no saint. Going into a second room he found more and even more beautiful apples. He began to eat them and forgot himself to such an extent that the strokes of midnight rang out and the mountain closed over him. To stay alive, the child ate his way through the apples and the pile went down until he found a figure carved in a piece of wood. That must be the saint! He rubbed the top of the wood and a voice spoke:

"What do you want?"
"I want to get out into the sunlight."

A moment later, the child found himself outside, still holding the piece of wood, which he rubbed to get everything he wished. He built a palace, where he lived with his mother, who had become thirty years younger. He travelled to Paris and quarrelled with the king, who tried to seize the lad's palace: but magic put paid to the king's army, and he offered the boy his daughter's hand in marriage. On the marriage night, the princess was surprised to see her husband put an old wooden figure of a saint on the hearth. A few days later the princess heard a hawker offering new saints for old (as they do), so she swapped the old wooden saint for a new plaster one, to please her husband. When he got back, the husband seized the new saint, broke it in two and went in search of the hawker. When he found him, he bought his entire stock, but when he rubbed the saint's head again, the saint told him:

"I can do no more for you. All your wishes have been granted until now, but it is time you learned to stop wanting things. I am going back to Roc Trévezel to await another eleven years to grant the wishes of someone else."

So if you happen to have a lad with you who is eleven today...

24.6 Guimiliau - A fine Parish Close

If churches and architecture are of interest, Guimiliau is for you. It is famed for its magnificent Parish Close of the 16th century. This, like all such parish closes, consists of a church, triumphal arch, a calvary and an ossuary (see the section Religious Brittany for more on this).

The calvary, one of the largest in the area, dates from 1580 and has over 200 figures including the story of Catell Gollet (Catherine the lost). Catherine was a servant girl, who did not confess all her sins to her priest. After this bad start, she went on to steal a consecrated host to give to her lover, who was the devil in disguise. She ended in hell and she is represented being tortured there. Catherine was used as a dreadful object lesson to terrorise the females in many a Breton flock. (Just to confuse you, there's also a town called Lampaul-Guimiliau just up the road which has another fine Parish Close.)

24.7 St. Thégonnec and the Wolf

Another superb Parish Close, one of the most complete in Brittany. Look out here for the carving of the saint with the wolf at his feet - the one he hitched to his cart after it ate his donkey.

25. Paimpol and Bréhat Island

An Interesting Coastal Outing

25.1 A Drive up the Coast

At the start of the day (or the end, of course, depending on which way you tackle it) are two beaches. The first is the **Plage Bonaparte**. It was from this cliff-hemmed beach, now a Mecca for those interested in the French Resistance, that between January and August 1944 and in 8 actions, 135 American and Canadian airmen, along with secret agents, were picked up by the Royal Navy without the German occupying forces' knowledge. It is reached by

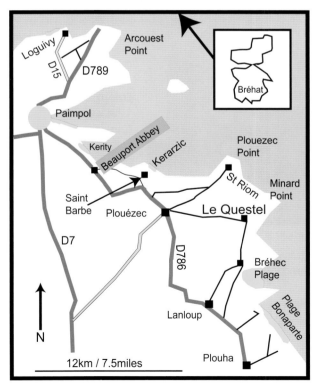

a pedestrian tunnel cut down through the cliffs. The next beach, the **Plage de Brehec**, is very good - and easier to get to.

To the south of Paimpol lies **Minard Point**, a spectacular view point across Saint Brieuc bay. A gun battery was positioned here in the old days against English raiders. The long distance coastal path GR34 (see the section 'walking in Brittany') runs here. There are outstanding panoramas.

On the way to Paimpol is the hamlet of **Sainte Barbe**, where there is another view point from which the islands and waters of the bay can be admired: as well as the geometrical forms of the wooden oyster platforms. There are hundreds of these, where oysters are farmed in the tidal zone. One can drive to the coast there and walk down to the small sand beach of **Kerarzic**.

Beauport , photo M. S-Kellinghaus, CRTB

Further towards Paimpol, you will pass the **Abbey of Beauport**. Dating from the 12th century, it is a romantic ruin in an attractive setting with rose gardens and orchards.
Open: Mid June to mid September, 10am to 7pm. Rest of year, daily 10am to noon, 2pm to 5pm.
Cost: Adult - 5€. Age 11 to 18 - 3€. Age 5 to 10 - 2€.

North of this is another sandy beach, at Kerity. There is also a town beach (sand) in Paimpol.

25.2 Paimpol

Paimpol. Population 9000. The Tuesday morning market, with fruit, fish, meat and shellfish, is recommended.

Paimpol is a bustling port packed with pleasure craft and, although much of it is modern, there are many fine old houses scattered throughout the town, especially around the **Place du Martray**. There are many fish restaurants.

The **Tourist Office,** place de la Republique, 22500, give a useful free map of the area and town.

    Open: mid June to mid September, Mon to Sat, 9.30am to 7.30pm,
    Sundays and public holidays, 10am to 6pm. Mid September to mid June,
    Mon to Sat, 9.30am to 12.30pm, 1.30pm to 6.30pm.
    Website: www.paimpol-goelo.com - in French only
    Email: tourisme@paimpol-goelo.com

Musée de la Mer - rue de Labenne. The museum of the sea is housed in a building which was originally constructed for drying the cod fished around Iceland. This building dates from 1880. The permanent exhibits concern the lives of the 'Icelanders' - as the fisherman who sailed from Paimpol to fish those northern waters were called - and also the environment they worked in. Light houses and beacons, coastal fishing and life on the high seas are covered. There are maritime paintings too. Often the temporary exhibits cover the work of a specific painter.

For opening times and admission charges, see below.

Musée du Costume - The costume museum displays the costumes which were worn at the end of the 19th and start of the 20th centuries during different stages of life. Baptism, childhood, communion, young girl, working wear, ceremonial costumes and widowhood. A particularly interesting point of the museum is the exhibition on the traditional Breton bonnet of this area between 1820 and 1930: how they were made and when they were worn. There is also a reconstruction of the main room of a house of the period. The museum is only open in July and August.

    Open: July and August - both museums are open every day, 10.30am to
    12.30pm, 2.30pm to 6pm. June and September - Costume Museum is
    closed, Museum of the Sea opens 2.30pm to 6pm.
    Cost: Sea museum. Adult - 4.30€. Age 7 to 18 - 2.10€.
    Costume museum. Adult - 2.60€. Age 7 to 18 - 1.35€. Joint ticket (both
    museums). Adult - 5.60€. Age 7 to 18 - 2.70€.

A Little History

The name of the town comes from pen (head) and poul (lake), so the name means the head of the lake – and, as the name suggests, once it had water to landward as well as seaward, making it virtually an island. Paimpol began to become important in the 15th century, when commercial cod fishing began. With the discovery of the new world, the fishermen migrated across the Atlantic during the season. Paimpol suffered badly in the Wars of the League 1589 - 1598 (see history section), being frequently occupied by English troops. The town grew In the eighteenth century to become one of the largest in Brittany. In the latter part of the 19th century Icelandic fishing began, which made the town's fortune. At its high point in 1895 the town had 80 fishing boats. A time of prosperity, but also a time of long separations. It took 1 or 2 weeks to reach Iceland, then seven months on the fishing grounds before returning: all this in often killing conditions of cold, snow and violent storms. 2000 fishermen perished at sea from the port. The Icelandic trade died out after the first world war. Every two years there is a festival of sea shanties in Paimpol (in early August, years with odd numbers).
to the North of Paimpol lies…

25.3 Arcouest point

Superb views of the bay and the island of Bréhat. Well loved by artists. From here one can catch the boat to the island (see below). There is a **Tourist Office** here.
   Open: Mid June to mid September, Mon to Sat, 9.30am to 12.30pm, 2.30pm to 6.30pm, Sundays and bank holidays, 10am to 1pm.

25.4 Bréhat Island

Population 400

The island, which is about 2 miles long by one wide, has important sea bird colonies and many wild flowers, indeed the southern island has a lush feel, with figs, eucalyptus and mimosa.

Many paths weave between the houses, leading to unexpected views which have inspired many a painter. Bréhat became famous at the end of the nineteenth century as a haven for painters and writers who came to search for inspiration in the purity of its light and the colours of the landscape. Now Bréhat's permanent population of about 400 is annually swollen to about 10 times that number in summer, when its three hotels are often fully booked. There are shops, eating places and a tourist information office here. You can also hire bikes. There are no cars. The only sandy beach on the island is at the **Plage de Guerzido**, about 300 yards from the landing spot. There are many islets around Bréhat.

Le Bourg, the only village, has charming stone streets, bars, pizzerias and crêperies. Although Le Bourg is touristy, the coast and landscape is wild, especially in the northern part of the island (the island is hour-glass shaped, joined in the middle by a bridge – well, sort of, there's no water beneath it…) There is a **Tourist Office** in Le Bourg.

> **Open:** July and August, 10am to 5pm (closed Sunday). April, May and June, Monday and Thursday, 10am to noon, 2pm to 4.30pm, Saturday 10am to 1pm.
> **Email:** syndicatinitiative.brehat@wanadoo.fr

Bréhat. Photo J.P. Gratien, CRTB

At one time the island was totally dependant on fishing – in fact they claim to have been the first to discover America (as many people claim that, of course, as churches claim to have a piece of the true cross, but their claim has to be as good as any). The lighthouse, Paon, on the northern tip, is about 2 miles from the southern tip, where the boat lands.

There are many legends associated with the island. Thus the lighthouse of Paon (destroyed by the Germans in 1944 and rebuilt after the war) is supported by two great rose- granite rocks, which are supposedly two men who killed their fathers, petrified by God.

The **Hole of Paon**, is a kind of well made of two granite blocks through which surges the sea. Young women would go there at low tide and throw a pebble in. If the pebble fell to the bottom without bouncing off the side, they would be married within a year: but each bounce added a year. Long haired 'little folk' with hats were supposed to share the island with mortal residents, like the elves and the shoe maker, rather disposed to help than hinder. Another tale is of a ghost, of Adelice Penquet who died in 1643, who came back to tell her friends that the island would sink under the waves, but only when God was no longer praised on the island. There is a glassworks in the former fort where you can watch jewellery, tableware and other artefacts being made.

Getting There
A ten minute trip from the mainland (Arcouest Point). There are about 16 crossings a day (half hourly) in high season.
> **Cost:** Adult - 8€. Age 4 to 11 - 6.50€. Bikes - 15€, including the cyclist.
> **Website:** www.vedettesdebrehat.com - has an English version.

26. Pléneuf to St Cast

A Coast of Great Beauty

The coast line described here is of an exceptional beauty with many fine views and excellent beaches, as well as a number of small and interesting towns.

26.1 Pléneuf Val André - Golden Sands

Markets: Tuesday morning at Pléneuf, Friday morning at Val André.

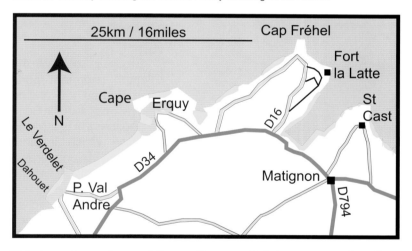

This town is made up of three villages which have grown together, Val André, created in 1860, Dahouet, an ancient Breton port, and the even more ancient Pléneuf (now the administrative centre). This beautiful area offers a great variety of outdoor leisure activities such as riding, windsufing (age 9 upward), sailing and golf. As well as having one of the finest sand beaches in North Brittany, it also has excellent walks along the coast in both directions. One way leads to the headland of Pléneuf and exceptional views over St Brieuc bay and Erquy. Here also is the bird sanctuary at Le Verdelet, a small island, accessible at low tide.

The island is a bird reserve sheltering a variety of seagulls, terns and cormorants. The other way takes you to the harbour of Dahouet, a typical, small Breton fishing port. In 1509, its sailors were the first to cross the Atlantic to fish for cod in the Newfoundland waters. Today the port harbours many pleasure yachts. There are boat trips from here to Bréhat island. There is a **Tourist Office**, at 1 rue Winston Churchill, who give out a good town guide (with English translations) with a map showing walks at both ends of the bay.

Open: Summer, Mon to Sat, 9am to 1pm, 2pm to 7pm.

Website: www.val-andre.org (has English version)

26.2 Erquy and the Cape

Market day Saturday.

Photo: J.P. Gratien, CRTB

Erquy is one of the most important ports in Europe for landing scallops (coquille Saint Jacques). It is also the place which inspired the unconquerable Gallic village in the Asterix tales. It has plenty of fine beaches (10!) to chose from, one of which is supervised. Over 20 restaurants/ creperies/ pizzas. A fine walk up to the **Cap d'Erquy** with its heathland and pink sandstone cliffs (but be aware, the nudist beach, the Plage de Lourtuais, is directly beyond it). Bikes can be hired in Erquy, as can kayaks and there are two mini-golf courses. The **Tourist Office** at 3 rue de 19 Mars have a useful town and cape map.

Open: Summer, Mon to Sat, 9.30am to 1pm, 2pm to 7pm, Sunday, 10am to 12.30pm and 3.30pm to 6.30pm. For the rest of the year it is closed on Sunday.

Email: info@ville-erquy.com

Pléherel (or Fréhel) Plage

Another good beach and a series of fine viewpoints as one approaches…

26.3 Cap Fréhel

It is a magnificent sight to look out from the top of this headland's steep, windswept cliffs across the largest area of coastal heath in France. The cape, 70 metres (200 feet) above the sea, with 300 hectares of heather and gorse covered heath is one of the most spectacular sites in Brittany. Sunset over the heath is also a feast for the eyes.

In good weather, the light from the lighthouse (the new one, the old one stands beside it) can be seen a hundred kilometres away: while from the top, the Channel Islands can be seen. The cave studded cliffs and seascapes are exhilarating. Falcons breed here.

Cap Fréhel, photo: E. Spiegelhalter, CRTB

26.4 The Wonderful Fort la Latte

La latte fort is a splendid and romantic fortress rising from the sea which has been featured as a backdrop in many full-length films (including Vikings, starring Kirk Douglas). The current fort dates from the thirteenth and fourteenth centuries, on the ruins of a fort which was built in 937 to defend the bay against ...the Vikings.

Open: Mid April to end September, daily, 10am to 12.30pm, 2.30pm to 6pm. Rest of year, weekends, 2.30pm to 6pm.
Cost: Age 12 and over - 4.30€. Age 5 to 11 - 2.40€. Under 5 - free
Email: Flalatte@aol.com

As well as oysters and mussels, which are farmed on this coast, more than 800 species of brown, red and blue algae, 90 types of molluscs and numerous species of birds have been recorded here.

26.5 Matignon

Has a good market on Wednesday mornings. The tourist office has local footpath guides and a leaflet in English about Matignon.
Email: tourisme@pays-de-matignon.net

26.6 St Cast le Guildo

A fishing port which specialises in scallops and clams. There are restaurants, brasseries, crêperies and bars, many shops and a supermarket. There are very fine views to be had here at the **Point of Saint Cast** - a superb view across the whole of the Emerald Coast (so named because of the colour of the water). There are two good beaches here, and fishing trips can be had. Enquire at the tourist office. Kayaks, windsurfing and catamarans can be hired.
Tourist Office, place Charles de Gaulle.

Open: July and Aug, Mon to Sat, 9am to 7.30pm, Sundays and bank holidays, 10am to 12.30pm, 3pm to 6.30pm Jan to June and Sept, Mon to Sat, 9am to noon, 2pm to 6pm.
Email: officetourisme@saintcastleguildo.fr

27. Dinard

How the Other Half Live

Population 104,000. The market , in the place des halles, is on Tuesdays, Thursdays and Saturdays.

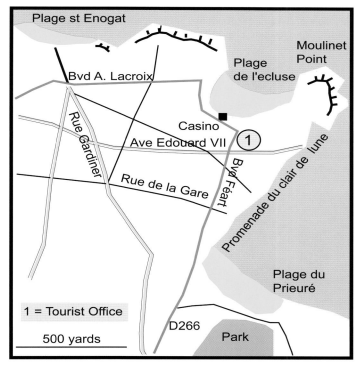

27.1 Dinard

Dinard is a luxury resort with wonderful beaches, seafront promenades, palm trees and gardens. It is popular with the jet set, especially British and Americans. It lies on the estuary of the Rance, one of France's prettiest rivers. The town stretches out over a succession of headlands interspersed by some very beautiful beaches. The coastal paths offer fine walking.

The **Promenade du claire de la lune** (moonlight walk) is one of the great Dinard classics. If you leave from the Général de Gaulle square, as soon as night falls, from June to September, you will be able to enjoy its musical atmosphere while walking along the seashore. A walk through the town itself, looking at the villas, is also an interesting experience. The **Tourist Office**, 2 boulevard Féart, 35800, gives out a useful free map of the town and area.

Open: July and August 9.30am to 7.30pm, daily. Rest of year, 9.30am to 12.30pm, 2pm to 6pm (closed Sunday in winter).
Website: www.ville-dinard.fr – in English and French

The best **beaches** at Dinard are the **Plage de L'ecluse**, the main beach, rather posh, bordered by luxury hotels and the casino, the **Plage de Prieure**, across the road from which there is a large and fine municipal park with a play area and animals (wallabies and lamas among others), and the **Plage de St-Enogat**. All beaches are under the surveillance of life guards during the season from 10am to 1pm and 3pm to 7pm.

Photo: J.P. Gratien, CRTB

Sea and River Trips

Many shipping line companies offer exploration trips of the Bay of Saint Malo, Cap Fréhel, Ile Cézembre (Cézembre island) or even a trip down the river Rance as far as Dinan. Ask for times at the tourist office.

A Little History

Dinard was a small fishing village until it was 'launched' by an American developer, James Coppinger in the 1850s. Then began a period of intense development and popularity, especially with the British upper classes and old India hands. With its soft climate, Dinard was described as "the Nice du Nord". The British even founded here the first French tennis club (1879) and the second French golf club (1887).

The first hotel went up in 1858 and dozens more followed, along with new roads, a casino and, of course, more grand "cottages," each more lavish and fanciful than the next. "There was every architectural style imaginable," relates the historian of the town, Henri Fermin, "from Italianate villas and Louis XIII pavilions to neo-medieval châteaux. And people didn't hesitate to mix genres and periods - the same house might have crenelated towers, half-timbers, stained-glass windows and granite stones. One villa was even covered with almost life-size statues of Breton saints."

By 1897, Dinard boasted 380 of these extravagant residences along with posh hotels. Adding to its mystique was the new name given to the entire coast from Cap Fréhel east to Mont-Saint-Michel: La Côte d'Emeraude. "While the waters off the Riviera might be azure," wrote Saint-Malo historian Eugène Herpin in 1890, "here they are a symphony of emerald greens". It proved to be an inspired bit of marketing. "Dinard became the leading resort in Europe," says Fermin. "Everyone who was anyone felt they had to be here - crowned heads of Europe, millionaires, celebrities." And of course, they expected to be entertained. Hotels obliged with elegant balls and concerts; some even brought in Parisian acts like the Folies-Bergère. But simply watching the local scene was high entertainment in itself. The beach was a veritable fashion show, and the streets echoed with the clip-clop of horse-drawn carriages - complete with livery boys - ferrying vacationing VIPs from one villa to the next.

The hub of Dinard social life was Montplaisir, the home of Philadelphia society matron Emily Hugues Hallett. "For 30 years, she was known as the 'Queen of Dinard,'" recounts Fermin. "Every evening she entertained princes and princesses, lords and ladies, counts and viscounts. Her parties would last all night, and she would sleep all day. No one ever saw her before five in the evening." The hedonistic goings-on were tempting fodder for caricaturists, who had a field day lampooning Dinard society.

27.2 The Tidal Barrage on the Rance

The 750 metre dam across the river Rance, which lies between Dinard and St Malo, was the first tidal barrage in the world and is still one of only two. The site, dating from 1961, produces electricity. As a renewable source of energy, it offers an excellent alternative to burning fossil fuels, and does not pose the dangers of nuclear energy. The estuary of the Rance, funnelling from the Atlantic, offers an ideal site for the harnessing of wave power, because of the massive tides, the second highest in the world, with ten times as much water flowing through the river mouth as does through the mouth of the Rhone. The Rance tidal power station can be visited (free), by appointment with the Tourist Office, from the end of June to Mid September.

27.3 Montmarin Botanical Garden

The garden is situated on the D114 between la Richardais (which is just south of the tidal barrage) and le Minihic sur Rance (further south). It is signposted from the D266 (Dinan to Dinard road), at Pleurtuit. A remarkable garden on the banks of the Rance. This shipowner's mansion looks out over a magnificent stretch of water. The 6 ha (14 acre) park, which is laid out in terraces leading down to the Rance, comprises a French garden and romantic park with lawns, groves, rockery, banks of trees and flowers and botanical collections.

Open: 1st June to mid September, 2pm to 7pm.
Cost: Adult - 5.60€. Age 14 to 18 - €4.60. Age 7 to 13 -€3.60. Under 7-free.

28. In and Around Dinan

History, Fun and Animals

28.1 Dinan - A Magical Town
Population 11,000. The market day, Thursday.

Dinan is wonderful. Set on a wooded plateau and surrounded by ramparts, it is easy to imagine how the town might have felt in the Middle Ages. Many of the buildings date from the 14th and 15th centuries, and the town is made even more pleasant by the abundance of trees and gardens in and around it.

A Stroll around the Vielle Ville
The old town is made up of half-timbered buildings, joined by cobbled streets, and at its very heart is the Tour de l'Horloge. A walk around the old town is a highlight of visits to so many Breton towns, but Dinan's really is one of the best.

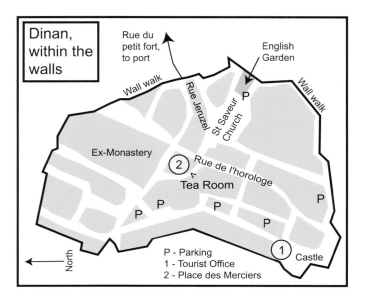

It is a good idea to visit the **Tourist Office** here first, 9 Rue du Chateau, 22100, as they issue a good free leaflet about the town, in English, with three suggested town walks, as well as more general guides to the area. Plus, of course, it will have information of what fetes and festivals are in progress or planned in this magical town.

Open: July and August, Monday to Saturday, 9am to 7pm, Sundays and bank holidays, 10am to 12.30pm, 2.30pm to 6pm. Rest of year, Monday to Saturday, 9am to 12.30pm and 2pm to 6pm.
Website: www.dinan-tourisme.com - (with English version)
Email: infos@dinan-tourisme.com

The Chateau. The castle houses an interesting small museum about Dinan and the area. The keep and the Coetquen tower can both be visited. The Tower was used for a time as a prison, known as the Dungeon of Duchess Anne. The basement is home to some evocative medieval tombs.

Open: 1st June to 30th September, daily, 10am to 6.30pm. 1st October to 31st May, daily, 1.30pm to 5.30pm. Closed 25th December and all of January.
Cost: Adults - 4.20€. Age 12 to 18 - 1.65€. Under 12 - free.

The impressive Gothic church of **St. Saveur** deserves a visit, if only for its place in Dinan's history. It contains the heart of Du Guesclin (see history section) - he has three tombs elsewhere for various other parts of his anatomy. It is said that it was built on the orders of crusader Riwallon le Roux, who vowed that if he escaped Arab imprisonment with his life he would build a church.

One of the best things about Dinan is its profusion of beautiful views. Not only is it a very pretty town, but there are plenty of places to enjoy it - and the surrounding countryside - from on high. **The Jardin Anglais** is one such place, a terraced garden on what was once the site of the St. Saveur Cemetery, and well worth a visit at any time of year for the plants and the view. **The port** is the best place to go for lunch, the restaurants there are cheaper and less tourist-focused than those in the centre, and it is a good area to explore. Both crepes and seafood are a good choice.

Climbing back up the **Rue du petit Fort**, You will pass the **Maison du Gouverner.** The Governor's House is one of the oldest houses in Dinan (15th - 16th century). An insight into a medieval interior.
Open: daily, June to September, 10am to 6.30pm.
Cost: Adult - 1.70€. Age 12 to 18 - 0.90€. Under 12 - free.

Return to the **Rue du Jerzual**, whose 15th and 16th century shops are now home to artists and craftsmen. Fascinating, whether you're in the market for souvenirs or not.

The Jeruzel, Photo: A. Bobrovirch, CRTB

The former **Franciscan monastery** on Rue de la Lainerie is now a school. The 15th century courtyard and cloisters can still be visited, and are a treat. Make sure to visit the **Place des Merciers** in your itinerary, for its pretty houses.

The **Musée de la Veilleuse** - Théière, 19 rue de l'Apport, is a marvellous tea room offering 60 varieties of tea, and specialising in Russian blends- the perfect place to finish the day. It also has a small museum displaying a variety of china, but the tea is the main attraction.
Open: Daily, 10am to 12.30pm, 2.30pm to 7pm.

The **Rue de l'Horloge** is a fine medieval street, and offers an impressive first view of the tower for which it is named…..

Dinan and Area

The **Tour de L'Horloge** (clock tower). Standing at 45 metres (140 ft) tall, the tower is the tallest building in Dinan and offers unparalleled views over the town and surrounding countryside, including the viaduct spanning the river Rance. The bell hanging in the tower, (and which still marks the passing of the hours to this day) was a gift from Duchess Anne in 1507, and is named after her. 158 wooden steps lead to the very top of the tower, from where a guard would have looked out for fires, unrest, or enemy advances.

Open: June 1st to September 30th, daily, 10am to 6.30pm. April 1st to May 31st, daily, 2pm to 6.30pm.
Cost: Adult - 2.75€. Age 12 to 18 - 1.75€. Under 12 - free.

Should you find yourself with some time left, or indeed a particular interest in trains, Dinan boasts its very own **Railway Museum,** located at the train station on the Place du 11 Novembre. It has some history about Dinan as a town, and a good deal about the history of rail in the area. The museum features many model railway layouts as well as an old signal box and posters.

Open: June 1st to mid September, daily, 2pm to 6pm. Mid April to end of May, and mid September to end of October, daily, 2pm to 5pm.
Cost: Adult - 3.80€. Age 12 to 18 - 3.05€. Under 12 - free.
Website: www.museedurail-dinan.com (in French only)

A Little History

The meaning of the name is unclear, but it may be from the Celtic 'Dunos' and 'Ahna'. Dinan then would be the hill of Ahna, the Celtic Goddess who protected both the living and the dead. In the 9th century, monks gathered here, close to an ancient Roman camp : while on another hill a castle was built as protection against the Saxons and later the Normans. It is shown on the Bayeux Tapestry. The fortifications were progressively strengthened through the centuries. The town's fortifications were put to the test in 1359 when it was besieged by the Duke of Lancaster. The day was saved when the town's hero, Bertrand Du Guesclin, took on an English knight in single combat and won the town's freedom.

The supposed site of the battle can be seen at the **Place du Champ**, and a statue of Du Guesclin stands in the square of the same name. Dinan today has blessedly preserved much of its ancient self and is one of the jewels of Brittany.

28.2   Cobac Children's Park, Lanhelin

Water slides, swimming pool, horses, little train, children's Island, boats, mini golf, animals, quad bikes, bouncy castles galore, rope

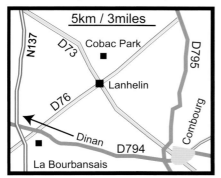

bridge and a large indoor games area. Snack bars and self-service restaurant.

Open: Mid June to end of August, 10.30am to 6pm. Exact dates for opening vary annually, so it's worth consulting the web or asking a tourist office.
Cost: Adult -14€. Age 3 to 14 - 12.50€.
Website: www.cobac-parc.com (with an English version)

28.3   A Zoological Park

The **Parc Zoologique de la Bourbansais** in Pleugueneuc is an historic estate of more than 100 hectares with a zoo with animals from all 5 continents: giraffes, tigers, lions, ostriches, zebras, panthers, lynx, pumas, monkeys, dromedaries and kangaroos. With a snack bar, picnic area and gift shop.

Open: 1st April to 30th September. Zoo and gardens, 10am to 7pm. Chateau guided tour (in French),11.15am, 2.30pm, 3.30pm, 5.40pm (and 1.15pm July and August).
Cost: Chateau (guided visit, in French) or Zoo and gardens, Adult - 14.50€. Under 12 - 10.50€. Under 3 - free. Both chateau and zoo and gardens, Adult - 18.50€. Under 12 -12.50€. Under 3 - free.
Website: www.zoo-bourbansais.com (with a page in English)

29. Saint Malo and its Bay

The Sea, the Sea

In a city that was once an island, the tides are naturally going to be very important to its people. They also affect the visitor too, as some of the town's attractions can only be reached at low tide. As such, it is best to **check when low tide will be** (any tourist office will tell you this) and plan your day accordingly. The itinerary set out below can just as easily be enjoyed in reverse, depending what time of day low tide comes.

29.1 The Grand Aquarium

This is at Saint-Servan, 3 miles to the south of the walled town (signposted from the N137 and from Dinard). The entrance fee includes an underwater ride on the Nautibus, past wrecks and a lost city. With a gift shop and restaurant.

Open: in season from 10.30am (9.30am Mid July – Mid August) till at least 7pm.
Cost: Adult -14€. Age 4 to 14 - 10€. Under 4 – free.
Website: www.aquarium-st-malo.com (has English version)

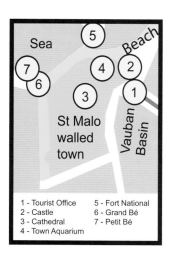

Sea
St Malo walled town
Vauban Basin
Beach

1 - Tourist Office
2 - Castle
3 - Cathedral
4 - Town Aquarium
5 - Fort National
6 - Grand Bé
7 - Petit Bé

29.2 The Town

Population 50,000 (200,000 in summer). Market days (within the walls), Tuesdays and Fridays, 8am to 1pm.

St Malo gets more than two and a half million visitors a year from all round the world. It is an international sailing capital and the biggest transoceanic races in the world start from the corsair city. The city belongs to the sea. Its wealth, past and present, is thanks to the sea, as it was a home to merchants, pirates and explorers.

It is really a fortified island, and was only joined to the mainland by a causeway in the 18th century. This isolation may explain the independent spirit of the 'Malouins', who associate themselves with neither the French in general, nor the Bretons (they say they're Malouins first, then maybe Bretons, and French if there's anything left). It is strongly recommended that you start at **The Tourist Office**, Esplanade St-Vincent, at the gates of the city. Firstly for **information about the tides** if you intend to go into the bay (see below), secondly for their **good maps** and thirdly for extra information about other attractions in and around St Malo. Should you be interested, they also have information about some guided tours in English.

Open: Daily, except Sundays in winter. July to August, Mon to Sat, 9am to 7.30pm. Sunday, 10am to 6pm.
Website: www.saint-malo-tourisme.com - has English version
Email: info@saint-malo-tourisme.com

Photo - M. S- Kellinghaus, CRTB

After entering the town, take a turn round **the ramparts** and enjoy the stunning views over the town and out to sea. It is from here that you can best appreciate the isolation and beauty of the islands in the bay. Staying in the 'Intro-Muros' (literally the area enclosed by the walls), visit the **Musée d'Histoire de la Ville**. Housed in the castle keep, which was built in 1424 by Duke Jean V of Brittany, the city museum is about Saint-Malo and its people.

Saint Malo and its Bay

It has been here since 1927 and has an informative section about the terrible damage that the town received in the Second World War, and its subsequent restoration.

Open: April 1st to Sept 30th, daily (except May 1st) 10am to noon, 2pm to 6pm.
Cost: Adult - 5.00€. Those in education, half price (military free!)

A **little train** runs around the town frequently (30 minute ride). It costs 5€ for 'adults' and 3.50€ for children (under 10's) and has a multi-lingual commentary. **The small Town Aquarium** of tropical fresh water was created in 1963 by Jean Grivet, a French naturalist (1917-1993). It is located inside a small curtain of ramparts linking Saint-Thomas Gate and the Queen's Fort, near the castle.

Open: July to August, daily, 10am to 8pm. Rest of year, closed January, Saturdays and Sundays in Feb, Mar, Nov, Dec, otherwise daily, 10am to 1pm, 2pm to 6pm
Cost: Adult - 6€. Aged 4 to 17 - 4€. Under 4 - free.

Photo CRTB

The Cathedral of Saint Vincent was built between the 11th and 18th Centuries. It wasn't definitively finished until the spire was fitted in 1987, long after the reconstruction of the town ended. Here you will be able to admire the magnificent group of contemporary stained glass windows.

There are a number of **Boat Excursions** which can be taken from St Malo, up the Rance to **Dinan**, out to the **Iles Chausey** or to the tiny **Ile de Cézembre** (700 yards by 200 yards), whose principal claim to fame is that it was, for 27 days solid, perhaps the most bombed and shelled, including napalm and phosphorus, piece or real estate in the second world war. When the Germans finally surrendered, their American captors presented arms to the survivors! Other boat trips go around the bay. Enquire at the tourist office for times and details of the trips.

A Little History

The town owes is name to a Welsh monk called Mac Low. It is said that he travelled for seven years in cold countries among the ice floes, in search of paradise, before landing at Cézembre, on the Emerald coast, around the 7th century. Canada and the Falkland Islands were both discovered by natives of the city. This explains the French and Spanish name for the Falklands, Malouines/ Malvinas. The wealth of the merchants of the city grew in part because of their sponsorship of the pirates who would raid Dutch and English boats and keep the loot. These raiding parties were also supported by the state - England's attitude to France being roughly parallel in the period. During the second world war, the town was 80% destroyed by Allied bombing. It was restored afterwards to its original plan (if only we had done the same to our bombed cities in Britain.) The 'joins' between the old and the new are barely visible. Dependent on the tides you can walk out and visit the various islands and forts in the bay.

29.3   The Bay

Keep an eye on the tides, which are the highest in Europe. They come in fast and high. You don't want to get stranded. Consult the tide tables before setting out and be sure to give yourself plenty of time.

The Fort National (10 minute walk at low tide across the sand opposite the castle) was built in 1689 by Vauban (yes, him again, see the entry about him elsewhere in the book), from granite from the Isles de Chausey. You will know whether it's open as its flag flies. An English speaking guide will lead you on a cruise with the Breton pirate Surcouf, or on a literary walk with Chateaubriand (see below). He will also tell you all about the epic story of the 1693 naval attack. While Americans and French considered Saint Malo "La Cité Corsaire," the English had another name for the port - "the wasp's nest." During the seventeenth century, Saint Malo grew rich off the profits of the privateers.

In 1693, the English converted a merchant ship into a floating bomb with which they hoped to destroy the city, but it exploded in the harbour and the only casualty was a cat. The fort was the spot where the local nobility were butchered after the revolution.

Open: from June - Sep, dependant on the tide.
Cost: Adult - 4€. Age 6 to 16 - 2€. Under 6 – free.
Email: fortnational@chateaux-france.com

At low tide, the very popular 5 minute walk across the sands opposite the walled town to the **Ile du Grand Bé** *(enquire locally about tides and advisability)* will take you to Chateaubriand's tomb, marked by a simple cross. From the Ile are great views of the main coastline.

François-René, vicomte de Chateaubriand was a writer and diplomat who is considered the founder of romanticism in French literature and Brittany's most famous writer. Chateaubriand (1768 – 1848) grew up in his family's castle in Combourg, Brittany. In 1791 he visited America which provided the settings for three of his romantic novels. As an aristocrat, he wisely absented himself from France during the revolution, in London. Returning to France in 1800, he later served as Ambassador to London and rose to be Minister of Foreign Affairs. His last work, **Mémoires d'outre-tombe** (Memoirs from beyond the grave), published after his death, is considered as his most accomplished work. Opinions differ on its quality, however. Karl Marx called it "the most classic incarnation of French vanité … the false profundity, Byzantine exaggeration, emotional coquetry … a never-before-seen mishmash of lies".

A further 5 minutes along the same spit of land, the **Fort du Petit Bé** hosts an interesting exhibition about the other forts in the bay and their construction, with a section about the tides, how they work and how they affect the area.

Open: From Easter to mid November, dependant on the tide.
Cost: Adult - 5€. Age 6 to 16 - 3€. Under 6 – free.

30. The Bay of Mont Saint Michel

Under Large Skies

Mont Saint Michel, wonderful though it is, is only part of what is to be seen around the bay. Here are some of its other attractions.

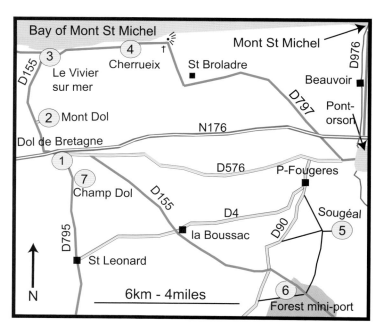

30.1 Dol de Bretagne

Population 5000. Market, Saturday morning.

Dol de Bretagne is the first, or last, town in north Brittany. It stands on a hill overlooking the bay of Mont St Michel. Indeed, the sea came up to it until the 10th century.

It is an important religious centre, being a bishopric and having one of the seven Breton cathedrals, a stop on the Tro-Breizh (see 'Religion in Brittany'). The **Tourist Office** is at 5 Place la Cathedral, 35120. They have useful free maps of the bay and town, as well as a very good map and brochure of Mont Dol (in French).

Open: July and Aug, Mon to Fri, 9.30am to 7pm, Sat, Sun & bank hols, 9.30am to 1pm, 2pm to 7pm. June & Sept: Mon to Sat, 10am to 12.30pm, 2pm to 6pm, Sun, 2.30pm to 6pm. May & Oct, Mon, 2pm to 6pm, Tue to Fri, 10.30am to 12.30pm, 2pm to 6pm, Sat, 10am to 12.30pm.
Website: www.pays-de-dol.com - also in English.
Email: ot.dol@wanadoo.fr

Photo, E. Speigelhalter, CRTB

The **Cathedral of Saint Samson** is an enormous structure, built of granite and dating from the 12th to 16th centuries. Although the outside is severe, the inside is impressive. There are several ancient houses around the cathedral.

A Little History

Dol was founded by Saint Samson, from Wales in the 6th century. It suffered greatly from Viking raids from the 9th century onwards – featuring on the Bayeux Tapestry.

It was the centre of Breton religious life for three centuries. Nominoe, who defeated the Franks, was crowned king here. It was a centre of Chouan resistance to the French revolution (see History of Brittany), and in the battle of Dol of 1793, 15,000 men were killed.

30.2 Mount Dol

Mont-Dol, a granite hillock which towers 65m (200 feet) above the plain, 2km North of Dol, is where legend has it that the Archangel Michael and Satan did battle. Satan is said to have been buried under the hill, and the foot print left by the Archangel when he jumped from the summit to Mont-Saint-Michael can still be seen in a rock. An interesting place. It's worth picking up the colour leaflet about it from the tourist information office at Dol. Around the mount stretch the fenland pastures of the bay; but they weren't always pastures. Until they were reclaimed by Dutch engineers, they were under the sea. According to legend the Bay was born following a tidal wave in 709 AD. The sea covered the then forest and drowned its villages. Only granite peaks such as Mont-Dol were spared. Thirty seven clock towers can be seen from here, as well as Mont St Michel and Granville in Normandy (on a clear day). There are some fine signposted walks here. Including a 13km (8.5 mile) one (shown on the pamphlet from the tourist office in Dol de Bretagne).

30.3 Le Vivier sur Mur

The Bay of Mont Saint-Michel, now a world heritage site, has the highest tides in Europe, an experience not to be missed. And they move fast – faster, it is said, than a galloping horse. As it ebbs, the sea reveals one of the largest areas of mussel growing and oyster farming in France, evidenced by thousands of wooden trestles and stakes.

Legend attributes the origin of these stakes, called bouchots, to an Irishman who was shipwrecked on the Charente coast in 1235. Sole survivor of this disaster, Patrick Walton stretched out nets at low tide to catch fish. He noticed that mussels attached themselves to the wooden stakes on which the nets were stretched. He then had the idea to plant stakes in a line to harvest mussels: the first bouchot was born. (The same phenomena is to be seen under wooden piers, of course). In this bay, mussel farming began in 1954. The activity developed quickly thanks to the favourable local conditions. Today, Le Vivier sur Mer and Cherrueix make up the biggest mussel farming area in France. If any more proof were needed of the cleanliness of the water, there are 25 to 30 seals in the bay.

Oyster farming: Photo, E. Spiegelhalter, CRTB

Guided walks are arranged from the Maison de la Baie. There are several different routes – you can visit beds of mussels or oysters, or wade out to a sand bank or a bird reserve. Forget about the galloping horses – the guides know the tides and also carry radio and mobile phones. There's even a tractor-pulled 'train'. There's a café here where you can get *moules frites.*

30.4   Cherrueix

The windmills here are reminders of the work of the Dutch engineers who reclaimed the bay from the sea. You can go sand surfing here. (Mon-Fri, 9 to 12, 2 to 6pm, Sat 2 to 6pm) on the fine sand. A training board costs 15€ an hour. You need old clothes and a robust pair of gloves. There are often road-side stalls in this area selling sand-grown vegetables, such as carrots, potatoes and garlic (indeed there is an annual all-day garlic festival here, usually on a Sunday in mid to late July). There is a fine view point at **Chapelle Saint Anne.**

30.5   Sougéal

Here there is a large marsh, and a bird hide, where migratory birds such as storks, ducks, shovelers, snipe and raptors can be seen. There are many geese here too and an annual goose fete (don't ask).

30.6   Miniature Port of Villecartier

For children and adults alike, a trip out for 15 to 20 minutes in one of 7 miniature electric boats (ferries, trawlers, tug boats, paddle steamers), on a lake in the middle of a 1000 hectare forest. The boats are 10-12 feet (3 to 4 metres) long and hold 2 to 4 people. Pedalos can be hired too. There are several walking trails in the forest. There is a bar/restaurant at the lakeside.

Open: July and August, daily, 11am to 7pm. April to June and September, weekends, 2pm to 7pm.
Cost: Age 10 and over (and adults) - 4€. Age 3 to 9 - 3€. Under 3 - free.

There is also an adventure park here – where one can go tree walking high in the trees on circuits of varying difficulty whilst attached by a safety harness to overhead cables.
It costs 20€ for an adult, 15€ for ages 10 to 13, 10€ for ages 4 to 9. I have not personally been there, so can not recommend it.

Photo, M. S-Kellinghaus, CRTB

30.7 The Menhir of Champ Dolent

This huge granite standing stone is 9.5m (almost 32ft) high, weighs around 50 tons, has been smoothed and shaped and has been standing here for tens of centuries. Here's one of the less bloody tales about the enigmatic pillar...

One day the devil, seeing Saint-Samson building the cathedral at Mont Dol, picked up a rock and threw it at the new edifice. He missed (didn't he always!) and the rock only destroyed the top part of one tower (still missing). The projectile landed several kilometres away, and is the menhir of Champ-Dolent. They say round here that it sinks into the earth an inch each year - and that when it disappears completely the world will end.

31. Mont Saint Michel

Marvel of the West

This day is extra! Mont St Michel lies beyond the river Cousenon, and is therefore not in Brittany at all, but in Normandy. However, since the Cousenon used to drift all over the bay until finally it was canalised by Dutch engineers, I'm sure the Bretons have a claim….

31.1 Mont St. Michel

The Mount is no longer an island. The water surrounding it has silted up over the years, and it is now reached by a road (the authorities are working to restore its insular status). But that does not detract from its wonderful, breath-taking impact. Mont Saint Michel is an eye-opening jaw-dropping marvel, from the moment that it looms above the flat bay until the moment you leave. A high place of western spirituality in a magical setting.

Occasionally, at spring tide, the parking area is covered by the sea, in which case you'll have to park on the causeway (some people park there anyway, so as not to pay for parking – but it can be a bit of a hike, and parking's quite reasonable, less than 5€ for a car, all day). It costs nothing to go onto the mount itself. The mount is a granite island, surrounded by massive walls, rising steeply to the abbey at its summit, which is crowned by a gilded statue of St Michael in armour, 152 metres (500 feet) above the sea. The steep street to the abbey is lined with an amazing collection of restaurants, cafes, posh shops, gift shops and cheap tat shops. It is, in season, a very slow shuffle forward through the crowds. The ramparts are magnificent, giving fantastic views over the bay (and they're free,). It is worth going up the street and coming back via the wall walk (or vice versa). The first way up onto the walls is in the corner, to the right, after the second gate.

Mont Saint Michel

Think carefully before taking a buggy onto the mount, as there are many steep steps up to the abbey and on the walls. You will probably end up carrying it for much of the time.

The must see is the Abbey, at the top of the street. This is an extraordinary building quite rightly called la Merveille – the marvel – as it soars sheer from the granite rock. As well as the Abbey and its rambling mass of associated buildings, atop it all there is a roof top cloister and garden, from which one can see the bay, far below. A leaflet is available in several languages in the price of the ticket. There are also guided tours in English, and Walkmans (Walkmen?). Both cost extra. No restaurant.

Open: 2nd May to 31st August, 9am to 7pm. 1st Sept to 30th April, 9am to 6pm. Last entry 1 hour before closing. Closed 01/01, 01/05, 25/12.
Cost: Adult: - 8€. Under 26 - 5€. Under 18 - free

A Little History

Saint Aubert's Dream
One night in 708, the Archangel Michael appeared in a dream to Aubert, the Bishop of Avranches, commanding him to build a church on the rock. Aubert didn't make things easy for Michael, who had to appear on three successive nights before the Bishop would listen to him – in fact the angel got so exasperated with the dozy prelate that he poked a hole in his skull with his finger! Go and see the skull – complete with hole – in the Eglise St-Gervais at Avranches - if you don't believe it. So Aubert had a chapel built on this site. The spot soon became a place of pilgrimage, which was renamed Mont Saint Michel (St Michael's Mount). The mount became part of the Duchy of Normandy in 933. From the 11th Century onwards the number of pilgrims grew as the incidence of miraculous events increased. With the pilgrims' donations, the monks built the abbey and many lodgings, workshops and offices for it, on the summit of the rock. At the end of the 12th century the abbey was home to 60 Benedictine monks.

In 1204, King Philippe Auguste of France took Mont Saint Michel by force from the Anglo/Norman King John, which caused much destruction. To make amends, he repaired the damage and constructed new buildings. Work on Mont Saint Michel seemed to be never-ending. During the Hundred Years War between England and France, the English laid siege to and attacked the island many times, but always to no avail. Mont Saint Michel remained impenetrable. It was the only place in Normandy we never took.

In the 16th century, the Mount began to fall into disrepair due to the lack of maintenance work and the decline in popularity of the monastic life. Protestant attacks during the wars of religion worsened the situation and by the end of the 18th century only a dozen monks remained. In 1793, revolutionaries transformed the abbey into a prison. In 1872, the restoration of the mount was entrusted to the care of the department for historical monuments For over a century, architects and conservationists have continued to improve and renovate the interior and exterior of the abbey.

31.2 Snakes in the Bay

Alligator Bay (formerly **The Reptilarium**) at Beauvoir (on the D976, from Pontorson to M.S.M. - see previous day's map) is quite a place, with 1000 square metres of displays indoors. There is a tropical house with 200 crocodiles and alligators. Then there are reptiles: boas, pythons, iguanas, monitor lizards and chameleons in a setting with tunnels, ladders to climb and glass pyramids. In the large gardens are 300 tortoises of 20 different species. The giant tortoises from the Seychelles islands can grow as long as 4 feet, the African spurred tortoises can weigh as much as 100 kg (17 stone) and live to be 100 years old. There is a shop, and a picnic area.

Open: 1st April to 30th September, 10am to 7pm. Rest of year, 2pm to 6pm
Cost: Adult - 11€. Age 13 to 18(and students) - 9€. Age 4 to 12 - 7€.
Website: www.le-reptilarium.com - partly in English.

The Breton Flag

The flag is nine black and white stripes, and a quarter representing 11 ermines. It was created by Morvan Marchal in the nineteen twenties, on the model of the Rennes arms and taking inspiration from the American and Greek flags. The 4 white stripes are for the 4 Breton-speaking dioceses, or "countries" (bro) Quimper, Vannes, Léon and Tréguier. The 5 black are for Gallo speaking dioceses (see the section on languages): St Brieuc, Dol, St Malo, Rennes, Nantes. The ermines are the arms of the Duchy of Brittany. The ermine is a small animal, like a weasel, whose fur has always been prized by the aristocracy. The 11 represent the kings and dukes who ruled independent Brittany. The Breton name for the flag is **Gwenn ha Du** - white and black.

Breton Geography

Brittany is the westernmost area of France, jutting out into the Atlantic. Its coast is wild, rugged and sinuous, stretching for more than 2,000 Kilometres (over 1,250 miles, one third of France's overall coastline).

Photo J.P. Gratien, CRTB

At 34,000 square kilometres, Brittany is slightly larger than Belgium. It has about 4,000,000 inhabitants: almost the same as the Irish Republic: and indeed Brittany and the Irish Republic have the highest birth rate in the European Union. Situated as it is on the western extremity of Europe, Brittany is exposed to the full force of Atlantic storms and can be wet and windy but, like Ireland, this climate creates a rugged colourful landscape and fabulous skies. Brittany falls into two parts, the **Armor** – the land of the sea - which is the coastal area, and the **Argoat** – the land of the wood – the inland area.

The Breton Departments

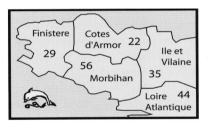

The division of France into 100 departments, each of about the same size, dates from revolutionary times, and is a sign of orderliness rather than a reflection of geography. Four of France's 95 mainland Departments (the other five being overseas) are Breton. These are Cotes d'armor (22), Finistère (29), Morbihan (56) and Ile et Vilaine (35). A fifth department, Loire Atlantique (44) is also, arguably, Breton. Two thirds of its inhabitants think so, anyway, although the state does not agree. For the purposes of this book, I have gone along with history and the majority and treat Loire Atlantique as part of Brittany.

The number plates of French cars include the department number. There are three groups on a number plate, a number, then letters, and finally a department number, for example: **6351 SZ 50** denotes a car from department **50** (Manche, in Normandy). Spotting and tallying them up can be a useful game to keep the kids quiet. It's a bit arbitrary to assign characteristics to the departments, but here goes anyway…

The five Breton departments are:

Finistère (29)

'The end of the earth.' (Penn-ar-Bed in Breton, meaning the head of the world). Finistère (or Finisterre) is the most westerly department of Brittany, and France, and, unsurprisingly given its remoteness from central France, the most Celtic of the departments. Its coast, all 795 kilometers (500 miles) of it, is sometimes high, wild and rugged and perhaps the lighthouse is the most distinctive feature of this dangerous coast. The danger is increased by the mists and fogs that this nose of France is subject to: but there are many, many superb beaches too. Here, the Iroise sea, between the islands of Sein and Ouessant, marks the transition between the Atlantic Ocean and the Channel.

Inland Finistère is also a superb place to explore with its natural sites, such as the Arrée mountains or the Black Mountains, and its rich religious heritage, the parish closes (see 'religious Brittany'). It is easy to find a pub with live traditional music of high quality, and one will often come across Irish or Scottish musicians playing with local bands. The city of Quimper (Kemper) is the capital and is well worth a visit. Morlaix, with its distinctive lantern houses, is also a fine place to go.

Côtes d'Armor (22)

(Aodoù-an-Arvor in Breton) carries a Gallic name. When the Romans invaded Gaul, the name of what is now Brittany and Normandy was Armorica. The name designated the people who lived near (ar) to the sea (mor). On a less romantic note, the name used to be Cotes du nord, but it was changed, as north coasts don't attract too many tourists. This is the least populous of the Breton departments, with most of the population living near the 350km (220 miles) of coast.

The Gallo/Breton linguistic and cultural dividing line (see the section on language) passes through the department, so that west of Paimpol it is more obviously Breton in language and culture. It has a superb coast with many fine beaches. The city of Dinan is unmissable.

Morbihan (56)

Mor-Bihan is Breton for little sea and refers to the almost landlocked sea below Vannes A very popular tourist destination, being on the south of the peninsula, with superb beaches, megaliths in great number (especially at Carnac and Erdeven) and some fine natural parks. Morbihan has 2040 hours of sunshine a year - that may be why the early inhabitants built granite dolmens and menhirs which point to the setting sun. Morbihan has many fine islands, ranging from tiny car-free gems, to the large and beautiful Belle-Ile.

Ile et Vilaine (35)

Home of the capital of Brittany, **Rennes**, and the incomparable town of **St Malo**. This is the eastern doorway to Brittany, and as such is home to some stunning fortresses, such as Fougères and Vitré. There are lots of recreational facilities for children in the area too, as well as the **bay of Mont st Michel**.

Loire Atlantique (44)

The capital of the independent kingdom was for centuries here, at Nantes. The administrative decision to cut Nantes from Brittany was taken by Pétain, in 1941 (see history section), and remains in force today. But most of the cultural organisations work on the historical Brittany, and Nantes and all its district are often involved in economic Breton activity. Apart from Nantes itself, there is much to see in this department, including excellent beaches such as **la Baule** and the fascinating areas of the **White lands** (salt) and the **Black lands** (peat).

The Sea, Lighthouses and Islands

The sea has always been at the heart of Breton life. All of the main towns, with the exception of its great eastern bulwark, Rennes, are on the sea or estuaries. That is because the sea has always been a highway, not a barrier, to the Bretons. The very name of their land, Petite Bretagne, Little Britain, is evidence that this was once the continental part of the Celtic peoples whose main home was the British isles. The seven remnant Celtic peoples (Ireland, Scotland, Wales, the Isle of Man, Brittany, Cornwall and Galicia in Northern Spain), all that remains of the culture that once bestraddled Europe, are all linked by the sea.

For the Bretons, the sea has been not only their highway, but their larder and a critical factor in war. The actual rise and fall of sea levels, linked to global warming and cooling over the ages, has also played a major role in the Breton (and indeed all mankind's) story.

Around 16,000 BC, the sea level in western Europe was about 350 feet lower than it is today. The English Channel was then completely dry and the Atlantic shoreline well to the west of its present location. Then, as the ice retreated, the sea broke through the low lying lands and isolated Britain from Europe. The sea level rose most rapidly between 10,000 and 5,000 BC, and stabilised at its current level at about the beginning of the Christian era.

As the builders of the stone circles were active during this period, some of their work is now under water. **Er-Lannic** double enclosure in the Morbihan Gulf (just south of Gavrinis island – see the day out at **Auray**) is a spectacular example of these shoreline changes: some menhirs now stand 1.5 metres below today's lowest tides. Given tidal levels, this means that the sea level was at least 6 metres lower than today when they were erected.

There are stories from many cultures, for example Noah and the flood, and Atlantis, which are doubtless related to these catastrophic rises in sea levels. Indeed, many regard the lost island of Atlantis as being somewhere in the English Channel: one German theorist even placing it firmly off the coast at Hull!

Given the central role of the sea in the story of Brittany, it is not surprising that the department has supplied most of France's greatest mariners, a very high proportion of its fisherman and much of its navy. The strategic value of dominating the sea lanes here is evident: to give just one recent example, more than two thirds of the submarines which the Germans based in France during the second world war were in Brittany (at Lorient, Brest and Saint Nazaire).

The actual coast of Brittany is not only subject to heavy sea traffic, but it is also hazardous because of strong currents and the presence of numerous islets and reefs, so there are lots of lighthouses. There are thirty of them in Brittany, 13 in the sea and 17 on land, all under the control of the Lighthouse and Beacon Department, founded in 1806 by Napoleon himself.

Several lighthouses can be visited, among them **St Mathieu** (see Le Conquet day out) and one on the island of **Ouessant** (see the day out). Another which can be visited is the tallest lighthouse in Europe, on the **ile Vierge** north west of Lesneven, in Finesterre (82 metres, 250 feet high). There is even a 50 mile (86km) lighthouse walk following the GR34 (coastal path) from Brest to Guisseny. Further information can be had from the tourist office at Brest (office.de.tourisme.brest@wanadoo.fr)

Brittany has many small islands - and some big ones too. Collectively, those Breton islands which are inhabited, along with two more further south, are called the **Iles du Ponant.** There is an interesting web site, www.iles-du-ponant.com (with an English version) which is dedicated to them.

The Breton islands offer a variety of landscapes and scenery: from **Ouessant** off the west coast, which in winter can be wracked by savage winds or wreathed in thick fogs (but in summer is a magical place), to the semi-tropical **Belle Isle**, or the island of **Houat** (see the day out in Quiberon), which is quite wonderful. What the islands have in common is that they are 'green'. There are few or no cars and a careful protection of the natural environment.

Many of the islands are covered in the days out in this book. Two days out (Ouessant and Belle Isle) are concerned purely with islands, while many of the other, smaller, islands are covered as parts of other days out.

Apart from visiting the islands, or the literally hundreds of superb beaches, there are lots of seaside things to do in Brittany: such as the **Port Museum at Douarnenez**, visiting the **Fortresses in the bay at St Malo**, a second world war **blockhouse at Camaret**, hiring surfboards or kayaks practically anywhere, taking **fishing trips from Concarneau**, visiting **a canning factory at Quiberon** or ordering fruit de la mer (shell fish platter), crabs, moules marinières or oysters at one of the thousands of fish restaurants. Then there are magnificent aquariums at **Brest**, **St Malo** and elsewhere.

The sea has shaped Brittany both physically and culturally: and it is very likely to shape your holiday too.

Breton History

It is worth reading this short account of the history of Brittany as just about everywhere that you go in the department, you will come across a part of this jigsaw. Seeing the whole broad picture should help you to put the bits in their place. Put in its simplest terms, Brittany's story is part of the big picture of Western Europe, whereby peoples have been pushed ever westward by successive waves of invaders from the east, and national boundaries have coalesced. The earliest human occupation of Europe which has left much evidence is the **Neolithic**, or new stone age (lithos being Greek for stone), when the standing stones were erected. The first constructions have been dated to around 5000 BC or a thousand years before the Egyptians built the pyramids. These standing stones are still to be seen in enormous numbers all across what is now Brittany, especially at **Carnac** (see relevant day out).

From about 1000 BC, the peoples of Europe were overrun by the **Celts**. It is an interesting if confusing fact that these people were also known as Gauls – so, even to this day, the French are described as 'Gallic' while the French for Wales is 'Le Pays de Galles' and the Irish are….Gaelic. The Celts ruled over most of Europe and parts of Asia (the Galatians of the New Testament). They even sacked Rome in 390 BC.

Though the Celts had no written language at the time, the Greeks and Romans discuss them quite a bit, usually disparagingly. The area which is now Brittany, as well as the Cotentin peninsula, was at that time called **Armorica** (land of the sea).

The Celts' appearance, at least, impressed the Greeks and Romans. They were often described as being red haired (although the people of Britain were described as small and dark-haired). Celtic women, upon reaching maturity, adopted a complex braided hair-style, and wore dyed and embroidered dresses. Plaids, or wrapped woven cloaks, were common for men and women alike, and wealthy Celts wore gold and silver rings and torques (arm rings). Brooches for fastening dresses and plaids were another common feature of Celtic dress.

Gallic men commonly spiked their hair and bleached it to an almost white colour with chalky water, and wore their beards long, while the Bretons and Picts tattooed their arms and faces with blue. Many Danish and English bogs have yielded archaeological evidence of cloth and dress, and Roman historians such as Tacitus also document some of the customs of everyday Celtic life. The Romans eventually conquered most of the Celtic lands, including Armorica, with Julius Caesar putting many of the people into slavery (see the day out at Vannes).

The sea was a highway for the Celts and there were many coalitions between British and continental tribes, especially against the Roman invaders. It is no coincidence that the French children's book, Asterix, which deals with Gallic resistance to Rome, is set in Brittany.

The religion of the Celts was druidism. The word "druid" is often cited as meaning "knowing the oak tree" and may derive from druidic ritual, which was, at least according to classical sources, performed in the forest. Certain areas were considered more charged with divinity than others, especially pools, lakes and small groves, which were the sites of the central ritual activities of Celtic life. (For more on this, read about the Nemeton in the day 'Locronan to Raz Point'.)

Caesar stated that the druids avoided manual labour and paid no taxes, so that many were attracted by these privileges to join the order. Having (and apparently wanting) no written language, they learned great numbers of verses by heart, and some studied for as long as 20 years. Their rituals were kept secret, although they appear to have held the oak and mistletoe to be holy.

The Celts believed in many gods. Roman sources say that they sacrificed people to them (and what appear to have been ritual sacrifices have been found in peat bogs). Celic gods came in threes, which probably, by adoption, explains the three parts of the Christian divinity as well.

According to Caesar, who gives the longest account of Druids, the centre of Celtic belief was the passing of souls from one body to another. It is clear that the Celts believed in an after-life, for material goods were buried with the dead. The Druids were finally overcome by the Romans in Anglesey, an island off the coast of Wales. Tacitus says of this: "On the coastline, a line of warriors of the opposition was stationed, mainly made up of armed men, amongst them women, with their hair blowing in the wind, while they were carrying torches. Druids were amongst them, shouting terrifying spells, their hands raised towards the heavens, which scared our soldiers so much that their limbs became paralysed. As a result, they remained stationary and were injured... at the end of the battle, the Romans were victorious, and the holy oaks of the Druids were destroyed."

The quality of the 'Peace of Rome' doubtless varied somewhat, depending on whether one was enslaved by the conquerors or collaborated with them – but at least it was a long peace. Roman rule continued until the 5th century.

The end of Roman rule in this area was caused, and followed by, great waves of attacks from Saxons, Angles, Jutes and other Germanic tribes. So strong were these in Britain, along with the raids of Scots and Picts, that many of the Romanised Celts of those islands fled to Armorica. So many of them fled that Armorica was renamed **Petite Bretagne**, 'Little Britain' as against 'Grande Bretagne', the islands of Britain. Bretagne it remains to this day, although the 'petite' has been dropped. In Great Britain, the invaders carved out their own new country, England, against fierce and prolonged resistance. The hero of that resistance was **Arthur**: and his deeds were sung across the Celtic kingdoms, in Wales, Brittany and Cornwall. Even in Richmond in Yorkshire, which was still Celtic then, his knights are supposed to lay asleep, awaiting the call to arms.

The Breton lands were ruled as a number of independent kingdoms, but not without struggle, for in Gaul, as in Britain, the Celtic people were pushed back by Germanic invaders. The most numerous of these were the **Franks**, from the area of modern Frankfurt. Their success reached its peak under **Charlemagne** (Charles the great), who ruled over an empire which encompassed most of modern France and Germany. In 851, after victorious Breton risings by **Morvan Lez Breiz** and **Nominoe** against the Frankish invaders, those invaders - now terming themselves French - recognised Brittany as a separate kingdom.

French control over their conquests weakened yet further in the years to come, and especially when a fresh wave of invaders came from the sea., the men of the north, or as they called themselves, **Normans**. These sea wolves landed on French soil and stayed, calling their beach head Normandy and advancing on Paris and the stronghold of the French. These last, under **Charles the Simple**, bought off the raiders by granting lordship over what had become part of Brittany (the Cotentin peninsula) to the Norman **Duke Rollo**, in 912. Maybe Charles wasn't so simple. He turned Norman ambitions against Brittany. Their war to possess it was to last for centuries.

Many Bretons joined with the Normans in the conquest of England in 1066. That did not stop Norman ambitions to take Brittany: and the wars against the land continued.

At first, the Norman/English were successful, with Geoffrey, son of Henry the second of England, appointed as Duke of Brittany. The war continued during **the War of Succession** (1312 – 1364) which took place between the children of the two marriages of Arthur, Duke of Brittany, who died in 1312. This war was fought to a large extent with English backing to one side and French backing to the other. It took place in a larger context during the **Hundred Year war** between England and France, which was essentially to decide whether England would keep her sizeable continental possessions (the English monarchs styled themselves 'kings of France' until the 17th century). Ultimately the answer was no. At the end of the War of Succession, the Duke of Brittany declared himself a subject of the French king.

A key figure in wresting their continental lands from the English was a Breton, **Bertrand Du Guesclin** (1320–1380). Du Guesclin, was a great soldier who did much to enhance the power and increase the possessions of the French king, Charles V. He was Constable of France from 1370 to 1380. He died while on a military expedition to Languedoc.

The end of a hope of Breton independence came with the almost unbelievably cynical and sordid manipulation of **Anne of Brittany** (1477–1514). The daughter of **Duke Francois II** of Brittany, Anne was heiress to the Duchy. Shortly before her father's death, a French army invaded Brittany and made the duke promise that Anne would marry only with the consent of the French crown. However, on her father's death Anne enlisted English and Austrian help to remain independent. In 1490 she married Archduke Maximilian of Austria by proxy. Besieged at Rennes in 1491, Anne was forced by the French to annul her marriage, and to marry Charles VIII of France. It was agreed that if Charles died before Anne had a child, she was to marry his successor. Accordingly, in 1499, she married Louis XII, who had previously obtained a divorce from his first wife. The marriage (1514) of Claude, Anne's daughter by Louis, to Francis of Angoulême (later Francis I of France) led to the eventual incorporation (1532) by France of Brittany.

Brittany was once again a scene of battle during the religious wars known as the **Wars of the League** (1589-1598). The opponents were those of the Protestant faith, which had renounced the authority of Rome and the Pope, and the Catholic faith (the League), which owes its allegiance to the Pope. Two Breton parliaments faced each other. Nantes backed the League. Rennes, on the other hand, sided with **Henri**, heir to the throne of France, a Protestant. The situation was complicated, as ever in Brittany, by foreign troops who lived off the country: English at Paimpol and Spanish at Hennebont. Before Henri became king as Henri IV, he became a Catholic, remarking famously that 'Paris is worth a mass'.

In 1598 Henri promulgated the **Edict of Nantes**, which guaranteed religious liberties to the Protestants and thereby effectively ended the civil war. One of the most popular French kings, both during and after his reign, Henri showed great care for the welfare of his subjects and displayed an unusual religious tolerance for the time. He was murdered by a fanatical Catholic.

Henri IV's descendent, Louis XIV, revoked the edict in 1685. It is estimated that two hundred thousand Protestants fled abroad, virtually depopulating many areas. The revocation of the Edict of Nantes weakened the French economy by driving out a highly skilled and industrious segment of the nation, and its ruthless application increased the detestation in which England and the Protestant German states held the French king. It also helped England's economy, in particular, bringing in many fine craftsmen, especially weavers and such influential families as the Lombards, Courtaulds, Flemings and Brunels.

Breton defences were massively strengthened during the 17th century against England, especially by **Vauban** (see the entry on Vauban).

In 1789, the first shots of the **French Revolution** can be said to have been fired in Brittany, when the French king abolished the privileges which had been given as a sop to Brittany at the time of its annexation. In the west of France, resistance to the revolution, and support for the deposed monarchy, gave rise to the **Chouans** (from chouette, or screech-owl, a cry which they imitated to signal to each other). Britain supported these attempts to restore the French monarchy - particularly with the landing at Quiberon (see the day out in Quiberon).

The Nantes to Brest canal was built between 1822 and 1842, so that shipping could pass through Brittany without being sunk by the British Navy.

The **Second World War** affected Brittany deeply. Politically, the most far reaching event was the removal of the département of Loire-Atlantique (including the city of Nantes) from Brittany to become part of the Pays de la Loire region.

Physically, the war shaped Brittany in the construction of defences on many headlands, and in the building of submarine (U boat) pens at Brest, Lorient and St Nazaire. It was the belief of the German naval commander, Admiral Donitz, that his U-Boats could, and would, strangle the life line from North America to Britain, starve Britain into submission and so win the war for his Fuhrer. He was very nearly right Churchill was to say: "The only thing to really frighten me was the U-Boat war." During the first year of the war, when only 6 U-Boats were deployed on patrol at any one time, they sank 4 million tons of the British Merchant Fleet. Successive Allied air attacks on the massively armoured submarine berths achieved nothing: and the towns themselves were blown to pieces by the American land armies, only surrendering after Germany itself had surrendered.

The **European Union** has helped modern day Brittany with large grants to improve its infrastructure. On a wider note, the same Union has gone a long way towards what is arguably its primary aim - defusing flash points between the peoples of Europe.

The above is a very brief précis of the history of Brittany. If you are interested in the subject, I can recommend **Discovering the history of Brittany** by Wendy Mewes, published by Red Dog books available through www.centralbooks.co.uk

Legendary Brittany

A Drowned City - The legend of Ys

They say that during the great March tide, Saint Guénolé's tide, the sea in the Bay of Douarnenez goes out so far that the remains of a town can be seen, the ruins of a palace, collapsed walls and the remains of stone causeways running into the sea... all that is left of the fabulous city of Ys.

Long ago Gradlon the Great, king of Cornouaille, had the marvellous city of Ys built for Dahut, his daughter. Because it was below sea level, Ys had to be protected by strong sea-walls. There was a lockgate to the port, and Gradlon alone would decide when the tide allowed it to be opened or closed. Now, Dahut, who was deeply attached to the ancient Celtic gods, accused Corentin, the bishop of Quimper, of having made the town a sad and boring place. She dreamed of a city where only riches, freedom and the joy of living would reign. So, she gave a dragon to the townspeople, which captured all the merchant ships at sea. Because of this, Ys became the richest and most powerful city in Brittany. Dahut reigned there as absolute mistress and guardian of Celtic heritage. Every evening she summoned a different lover to the palace, obliging them to wear a silk mask. But the mask was enchanted and at dawn it turned into metal claws, killing the lovers, whose bodies were then thrown into a chasm (see the day out in Morlaix for their eventual destination).

One fine day a prince, dressed all in red, arrived in the city. Dahut immediately fell in love with him. Now, it was really the Devil sent by God to punish the wicked town. For love of him, Dahut stole the key to the lockgate from her father while he was asleep, and gave it to him. The prince opened the lockgate and the ocean in all its fury rushed into the town; drowning the horrified inhabitants.

Only good King Gradlon succeeded in escaping, with the help of Saint Gwenolé. On his horse he waded painfully through the waves, weighed down by none other than his daughter. At the saint's urging, the king threw off his daughter and managed to reach the shore. To this very day, when it is calm, the fishermen of Douarnenez often hear the bells ringing under the sea. They say that one day Ys will be reborn finer than ever, because it was only flooded. Dahut, it is said, became a mermaid, and will only regain human form when the city rises again.

It is also said that the city of Ys was the finest capital of the world and that the city of Paris got its name because "Par Ys" means "like Ys" in Breton. Two popular Breton proverbs testify that:

Abaoue ma beuzet Ker Is, N'eus kavet den par da Paris
Since was drowned the City of Ys, Never has Paris been its equal

Pa vo beuzet Paris, Ec'h adsavo Ker Is
When Paris will be engulfed, Will re-emerge the City of Ys

The story is a very interesting one in that it echoes many tales of drowned towns in the western lands, not least Atlantis. With the rising tides that cut Britain off from the continent several thousand years ago, many coastal settlements were lost to the sea, some, doubtless, overnight. There are also interesting allusions here to the breaking up of belief in Celtic Gods, and the blackening of their character by the Christians.

Korrigans
When one people invades another, the invader tends to cast the conquered in the role of the villain: one needs to think no further back than the white invaders of America and the 'Red Indians',

but the habit is much older than that. The Iron Age people cast the Stone Age people that they supplanted as spirits and witches who were afraid of iron. The Christians made the old gods afraid of their cross, and so on. In the past, Brittany was swarming with supernatural and often malevolent creatures, and the Bretons feared them as much as they delighted to tell of them. Korrigans, gnomes who resemble small humans, hide beneath rocks, in the undergrowth, in fields or near menhirs and dolmens. These, like pixies in Cornwall, are made much of in Brittany.

Mermaids and Morgans
Nymphs and water sprites make their homes near fresh water rivers and lakes throughout Armorica. Mermaids - beautiful, fishtailed women - are said to live along the coast. These are the sea people known as the Morgans (Morganezed in Breton). Again, there are echoes here of rising waters and drowning cities – and Arthur too, for was not his evil half sister Morgan le Fay?

Their harmonious songs can be heard between Saint-Cast and Quiberon, or on the islands between Bréhat and the Gulf of Morbihan. With their naked bodies and long blonde hair, entangled with seaweed, they entice sailors down to their coral and diamond palaces, where the sailors drown. Some of the mermaids are extremely evil, causing ships to smash against rocks or dragging children into the sea.

King Arthur
The first written Celtic records date from the 6th century and these are very few. In Great and Little Britain, the tales of King Arthur are without doubt based on the fights of the Celts against the Germanic invaders from the east and north.

The first mentions of Arthur, in Welsh, are shadowy, the earliest of them (The Gododdin, c594), seems to suggest a link with Arthur's Seat, in Edinburgh and tells of a catastrophic defeat, probably at Catterick, in Yorkshire. Arthus is referred to in these earlier references not as a king but as a duke, giving rise to the theory that he was a Celtic nobleman at the end of the Roman occupation.

His death at the battle of Camlann (Somerset?) when combat began between the two facing forces because a soldier drew his sword to strike a viper, is a key image.

In the preface to the Legend of St. Goeznovius, the Breton writer, William, Chaplain to Bishop Eudo of Leon, gives an amazing, capsulized history of King Arthur. This dates from 1019 (although the date is disputed) and is the first known Breton written record of Arthur, including his wars in what is nowadays France.

In AD 1133, Geoffrey of Monmouth wrote a work on British history which introduced Arthur. Geoffrey, however, was hardly a reliable historian. The superb historian Gibbon wrote on Arthur with his usual wit: "During a period of five hundred years the tradition of His exploits was preserved, and rudely embellished, by the obscure bards of Wales and Armorica, who were odious to the Saxons and unknown to the rest of mankind. The pride and curiosity of the Norman conquerors prompted them to inquire into the ancient history of Britain; they listened with fond credulity to the tale of Arthur, and eagerly applauded the merit of a prince who had triumphed over the Saxons, their common enemy."

At any rate, Arthur is 'the matter of Britain', no less so in Little Britain than Great Britain. The Paimpont forest is particularly associated with the Arthurian cycle in Brittany (see the day out 'Josselin and Paimpont').

Tristan and Isolde
Tristan is first recorded in writing in 1120, although the tale itself is almost certainly much older. Tristan and his tale, and even the spelling of his name, vary from poet to poet.

Beroul, a Norman writing in the late twelfth century, tells of Tristan going to Ireland where he slays a dragon and brings back the fair Yseult for his uncle King Mark to marry. Along the way, they accidentally drink a love potion that causes the pair to fall madly in love for three years. Although Yseut marries Mark, she and Tristan are forced by the potion to seek one another out for adultery.

Although the typical noble Arthurian character (actually, the story predates the Arthurian tales, but was later incorporated into them) would be shamed from such an act, the love potion that controls them frees the couple from responsibility. Thus Beroul presents them as victims. The king's advisors constantly try to have the pair tried for adultery, but again and again they use trickery to preserve their facade of innocence. Finally the love potion wears off, and the two lovers are free to make their own choice as to whether they cease their adulterous lifestyle or continue. Beroul's ending is morally ambiguous. In the 19th century, Richard Wagner composed the highly acclaimed opera Tristan and Isolde.

It was the thesis of French mediaevalist Joseph Bedier that all of the Tristan legends could be traced to a single original poem, translated into French from an original Cornish or Breton source, with Tristan then being Drustanus. The Welsh recorded his name as 'Trystan.' I have read that a standing gravestone near Fowey in Cornwall says in Latin 'Drustanus Hic Lacit Cunomori Filius' (Drustanus lies here, of the house of Cunomorus). Cunomorus is the Latin name of King Mark of Cornwall, who was, of course, Tristan's uncle.

The feeling of magic in the Celtic fringe lingered very late. In living memory, fairies were believed in and perhaps they still are. It is certain that the old standing stones are still used to aid fertility.

The Breton Language

Nantes and Rennes are part of High Brittany (Breizh Uhel), the eastern part of the country, where the language was never Breton, but Gallo, a language based on Latin. Lower Brittany (Breizh izel), the area roughly to the west of a line from St Brieuc to Vannes, is where Breton was the chief language. At the beginning of the 20th century, 3/4 of the Lower Breton population spoke Breton only, half of them did not speak a word of French (of a then population of 1.5 million). Today, if Breton and Gallo are still in use, French is spoken everywhere in Brittany. Many people in Lower Brittany can't speak Breton, and quite a few Breton speakers, or learners, live in High Brittany. There are no more Breton-only speakers, but there are 240,000 bilingual Bretons.

The Celtic languages fall into two groups: the Goidelic, or Gaelic (Irish and Scottish) and the Brythonic or British (Welsh and Breton). Breton, then, is closely related to Welsh (although not that close, while some Welsh and Breton speakers report that they can understand each other reasonably easily, others say they can not.)

The language, like Welsh in Great Britain, was for many years banned in schools and only recently has it been seen by the authorities as anything but backward and divisive.

A Few Breton Words

Aber, aven: estuary (Aber-Wrac'h, Pont-Aven)
Amann: butter
Ankou: death
Aod (aot) : coast, shore
Argoad, argoed (argoat, argoet): wooded land, inland
Armor/ Arvor: coastline
Avel: wind
Beg (bec): point, top, summit
Bihan (bian): small (Enez Vihan: small island)
Bras (braz): large (Mor-Braz : the Ocean)
Breizh: Bretagne (cf. the BZH sticker on many cars)
BZH, very frequently seen, stands for Breizh, which is the Breton word for Britanny (written with the Peurunvan spelling system). (Mor-Breizh: the channel)
Bro: country/land
Du: black
Demat: Good day

Enez (inis): island (Enez Du: Black Island. Note Inis Mon - or Mona - is the Welsh for Anglesey)

Fest-deiz: Day festival

Fest-noz: Night festival

Gallaou: A French person, a Gaul

Goat (or coat or goët etc.) means a wood, as in Huelgoat, argoat, the wooded lands

Gui- a hamlet.

Gwenn (guen): white, sacred (Feunteun Gwenn: pure fountain)

Kastell: château, fortification (Plougastell: château parish)

Kenavo: goodbye

Ker (or Kuer or Guer): town, village, hamlet

Kozh (koz, koh, cos, coz, co-): old

Lan: hermitage, monastery (Lanildut)

Lann: moor

Loc: isolated place, hermitage

Loc'h : lagoon, coastal lake

Men: rock, stone

Menez (mene, mane, mine): mountain (Ménéguen : white sacred mountain)

Meur: grand, important

Mor: sea (Mor Bihan: little sea)

Nevez (neue, newe, neve, nehue): new

Nozvat: Good night.

Palud: marsh land

Penn: head, end, summit(Penn Ar Bed : Finistère)

Plou (plo, plu, pleu, ple, pli): parish – often with a saint's name

Roc'h (roch, roh): rock

Saoz (i.e Saxon): English person

Ti (ty): house

Treizh (treiz, treh, trech, tre): passage

Tro- or Traou: a valley

Religious Brittany

Brittany is famous for its churches, its parish closes and its religious processions – which are called *Pardons*.

Dating mainly from the fifteenth to the eighteenth centuries, the **parish closes** are mostly situated between Landerneau and Morlaix in Finistère the most westerly department. Each village competed to have the most important grouping: the highest tower, the most monumental arch or the calvary with most figures. They are often totally out of scale with the small towns and villages in which they are built. The closes (French **enclos**) all have several factors in common: a triumphal gate, a cemetery, a church, a charnel-house (ossuary) and a calvary. The close is a sacred place and is regarded as the link between the world of the living and that of the dead.

The **triumphal gate** often has several arches generally decorated with statues. There is a **cemetery** in the parish close. Since the size of the cemetery is limited, the remains of the dead were regularly removed from the tombs in order to save room. The bones were placed in a special building called a charnel-house or **ossuary** (ossuarie). This, in turn, was also emptied when it was full. The **churches** often contain unsuspected treasures, astonishing rood screens, truly beautiful stained glass windows, moving votives, sumptuous organ cases but most of all, astonishing statues of saints.

A **calvary** is a granite monument with statues of Christ on the cross and various personages from the bible. It recounts biblical episodes and in former times was used by curates for religious instruction. The calvary is in some ways the development of the wayside crosses encountered in their thousands throughout the Breton countryside. The most spectacular Finistèrian calvaries are:
Guimiliau, with more than 200 figures depicted on two levels (1581-1588).
Saint-Thégonnec (1610).
Plougonven (1554).
Pleyben, with 28 episodes of the life of Christ (1555).

(A reference to Pleyben from a long-dead book for some reason tickles me greatly: "On September 24th, 1904, at the parish church of Pleyben in Brittany I noted a splendidly carved and gilded aumbry of wood on the north wall near the High Altar." *Ceremonial Curiosities and Queer Sights in Foreign Churches*. by Edward J. G. Forse. London: The Faith Press, 1938.)

There are three very popular tourist circuits of the parish closes, consisting of 8, 13 and 18 closes. The leaflets for these are widely available in tourist information offices. However, except for a dedicated 'church bagger' this is ecclesiastical overkill, so I have chosen two for the day out '**Finistère, an inland journey**.'

The **Pardon** is the expression of popular devotion to a particular saint, from whom grace or a pardon is requested. These ceremonies normally take place once a year. The solemn mass is followed by a procession of singing villagers in the traditional costume (a black dress and lace apron and cap for the women) with banners, relics, statues and crosses. The ceremony terminates with a secular fête, involving dancing, music and traditional games.

The ceremony of the **Pardons of the Sea** is a little different, since once the procession arrives at the port, the clergy, children and reliquaries go on board a boat. The Priest then blesses all the vessels in the port, as during the pardon of Saint-Jacques at Locquirec (on the north coast of Finistère - last Sunday in July).

The most important pardon is that of Anne, patron saint of Brittany, which takes place at **Sainte Anne d'Auray** (just north of Auray, near the south coast). It takes place on the 26th of July each year and is attended by 20,000 people.

The Great Pilgrimage (Tro Breiz)
To honour the seven founders of Christianity in Brittany, the practice seems to have spread from the 12th century onwards of undertaking a tour of Brittany (Tro Breiz) to visit their tombs, each in its own cathedral. Saint Patern is venerated in Vannes, Saint Corentin in Quimper, Saint Pol Aurélien in Saint-Pol-de-Léon,

Saint Tugdual in Tréguier, Saint Brieuc and Saint Malo in the towns named after them and Saint Samson in Dol-de-Bretagne. During the 14th and 15th centuries many thousands of pilgrims would make this journey on foot as an act of piety and reverence once in their earthly life. Any Breton who did the Tro Breiz was sure to go to Paradise; any who failed to do it during his lifetime was condemned after his death to carry it out by advancing the length of his coffin every seven years.

The 370 mile Tro Breiz gradually lost its appeal from the 16th century onwards after the wars of religion called the Wars of the League (see the history section). According to Jaques Cambry, in 'Voyage en Finistère' (1794), it was by then a scene worthy of the brush of Brueghel: "People... buy crosses, rosaries and images that they touch to the statue of the half-god; they rub their knees, their foreheads, their paralysed arms against a mystical rock; they throw farthings and pins into the fountains, they wet their shirts to be healed, their belts to give birth easily, their children to make them immune to pain. They dance and leave intoxicated, emptied of money but full of hope... don't you find in these superstitious practices a less civilised era?"

However, after almost falling into disuse, the Tro Breiz has now been updated. As a spiritual and cultural tour, it can be enjoyed by bike, on horseback, by car or coach.

Breton Saints
Brittany has more saints than any other part of France. There are hundreds of them and their painted statues adorn chapels and churches everywhere. In fact, very few have actually been recognised by the Vatican authorities (it was only in the twelfth century that the creation of saints became a papal monopoly).

Breton saints are often credited with powers that obviously originate in earlier Celtic beliefs. So St-Triphine is invoked at Tréal to bring rain, while at Glénac St-Leon brings good weather if an offering of red flowers is made. St-Venier at Langon makes the milk of nursing mothers flow, and St-Meen has the power to cure skin diseases. There are saints who are invoked on all occasions, whereas innumerable others are invoked against specific ailments - rheumatism, baldness, etc. Even horses and oxen have their own saints - St-Cornely and St Herbot.

Druidism Lives On?

Christianity was established in Finistère at the same time as the rest of Brittany: but the locals, who had cast off 400 years of Roman civilisation with hardly a trace, were stony ground for the missionaries. Inroads were slowly made, but at the end of the peninsula – to the west of Brest and in the western islands - paganism was still recorded in the 17th century. Even when converted, the Breton of Finistère made Christianity mould itself to druidism. The new religion put its crosses on menhirs, its chapels and churches (almost all of them) on holy springs.

The priestess of the Goddess Koridwen have long gone: but the Korrigans remain. Saint Anne, the patron saint of Brittany, is, in the Christian religion, the mother of Mary, the mother of Jesus. Ana, in Celtic religion, was the mother of the Gods. The mistletoe is no longer cut on the sixth night of winter with a golden scythe, but it retains its religious significance. It is the plant of the cross, it cures fevers and gives strength. People kiss beneath it.

Mid-summer's day may have become Saint John's day, but the fires are still lit, and they are still kindled from oak.....

Walking in Finistere

France is well served by a number of Grandes Randonnées – long distance footpaths. A full list of them can be had (in several languages) at www.gr-infos.com Boards sign posting them, for instance 'GR34', are often to be seen. The following has been written by Wendy Mewes. More about Wendy at the end of this piece...

Finistère is a walker's paradise, with the most unexpected and varied terrain in Brittany. Whilst the famous GR34 coastal path is well-known, the interior has many surprises to offer. Half an hour from Roscoff is the heart of a wild land. On the barren heights of the Landes de Cragou wolves ranged freely a hundred years ago and wild boars still inhabit this relatively unpopulated area.

Little used tracks criss-cross the Monts d'Arrée with their sharp granite outcrops affording spectacular views from the Channel to the Black Mountains in the south. These peaks, none over 400m, are yet impressive in contrast with the tracts of tourbières (peat bogs) and the Reservoir of St-Michel which they surround. An 18km walking trail encircles this eerie lake, crossing the marshes on wooden walkways. It is the scene of many Breton legends of nocturnal washer-women luring travellers to their doom or Ankou, the Grim Reaper, driving his cart in search of lost souls. At nearby Mougou Bihan, the short ecological Korrigan Trail starts from a fine alley-grave (c.3000BC) and can form the beginning of an adventurous trek onto the rough ridges above. Further east around Huelgoat lie the lingering remains of the ancient wooded coverage of Brittany. Here there are walks of exceptional beauty through the glorious forest, following 18th century canals out to the old lead/silver mines exploited since Roman times or climbing to an Iron Age earthwork, romantically known as the Camp of Arthur.

A detour of a couple of kilometres can take in the standing stone of Kerampeulven, typical of the Neolithic remains which litter this landscape. By contrast, the natural phenomenon of the granite Chaos is also an unmissable experience, with the River Argent tumbling round and tunnelling through granite rocks of fantastic shape and size. This region has something to offer walkers of all ages and abilities and there is more than enough variety to make it the perfect base for a walking holiday.

Wendy's book, **Walking in Finistère** (**ISBN**: 0953600130) is published by Red Dog Books. Wendy also runs **Wildwalks**, which provides guided walking for groups or individuals on request, in addition to a programme of regular walks which are open to all. For details see Wildwalks on www.wendymewes.net or email wildwalks@wanadoo.fr

Cycling in Brittany

Being an occasional cyclist myself the pleasures of cycling in France are very real for me: and I mention them on the day out covering the isle of Ouessant. However, there is more to cycling than day rides. A whole holiday can be had on a bike, either camping or staying in hotels. I am no expert on such a holiday: so will merely quote from an English couple, Kate and Geoff Husband, who run cycling holidays in Brittany (details at the end of this piece)…

Anyone who has ever cycletoured in France knows exactly why this large European country is the 'Mecca' for cycletourists coming from all over the world. Not only is cycling the national sport, but it is one that has a presence throughout the country. Local people are used to seeing cyclists every day, are quite likely to cycle seriously, or at least know someone who does, and so the image of cycling is hugely positive rather than being 'poor man's transport'. The result is that drivers are used to giving room to cyclists, that turning up in a bar or small restaurant in Lycra, dripping with rain, doesn't get you asked to leave (as can happen elsewhere) and that as a cyclist you are viewed with interest and friendliness.

Of course cyclists have other 'requirements', primarily food and somewhere to stay. Food in France? Though no cyclist is going to be impressed by a peeled prawn, sprig of dill and an artistically pooled drop of red sauce, the curse of 'Nouvelle Cuisine' is hardly likely to be encountered by the average cycletourist. In the countryside you'll find small 'ouvrier' (literally "worker's") restaurants that for 10€ will provide a four course meal, often with wine and coffee, that you couldn't cook yourself for that money! Evening meals aren't much more and of course the range of fresh food is enough to keep you in picnics for a lifetime. And the wine - it's amazing just how good a 1.50€ bottle can be: **especially when you feel you've deserved it**.

Then there's the range of campsites. Even if you've never camped before it's worth doing at least one cyclecamping trip in France and wondering at the wealth of cheap municipal and private websites covering the country. For those looking for a bed for the night most small towns will have hotels where a simple but good room will run at around 40€ per night, making it easy to piece together a tour on an on-the-fly basis.

So much for France. If you cycle in Brittany, it gets even better! Brittany has the most spectacular and varied coastline in France, with sweeping kilometres of golden sand one minute, rocky coves and cliffs the next.

Inland you'll find lakes and forests linked by canals, (notably the 172 mile Nantes-Brest canal) all of which have towpaths perfect for cycling. In the heartland of Brittany there is little intensive farming so you are left with small fields, tall hedges with magnificent trees and of course the remnants of the great Pan-European forest are everywhere.

The landscape is littered with stone-age monuments, ancient Celtic churches and all this linked by a maze of tiny lanes where a car per hour is the norm. Low intensity farming exists in harmony with the countryside, butterflies abound and the dawn chorus has to be heard to be believed. The verges are full of flowers, the rivers and canals teem with fish and in the forests you may see foxes, deer or, if you're lucky, wild boar. In a car you miss so much of this.

Even in the darkest depths of the interior you will pass a watering hole every few kilometres where the locals will shake your hand and smile at your loaded bike. The villages often still have small shops, bakers and bars: while the larger ones often have a tiny hotel, perhaps with half a dozen rooms, or a campsite by a lake maintained by the commune to attract passing visitors. And yet this heartland of Brittany is ignored by almost every tourist. Yes go to the south coast in August and it'll be busy, but 10 kms from that coast you wouldn't be able to tell the difference between April and August.

On a bike you can go at your own pace, stop where and when you like and soak up the sights and sounds of this wonderful part of France. Yet in a week you can cover a large area, to the coast and back or around the quiet heartland. In a fortnight, you can take in both north and south coasts with ease. And it's good for you – and it makes you feel good too (most of the time!)

Kate and Geoff Husband have been running Breton Bikes since 1989. Their prices are very reasonable. You can have a weeks cycle camping from 225€, including all hire, and a weeks hotel based bike touring from around 500€. To find out more about them and their routes, see www.bretonbikes.com, email info@bretonbikes.com or phone for a brochure: UK (00 44) 01578 350 379, France (00 33) 2 96 24 86 72.

Vauban, 1633-1707

Sebastien le Prestre de Vauban is without doubt the best known French military engineer; and perhaps the most influential in the world, as his disciples adopted his methods and often his plans to build 'a la Vauban.' Vauban was born in what is now the department of Yonne, in central France. During his military career, he built 33 forts and town walls, and strengthened 300 others – principally in the north of France, but also all round the coasts and borders of the country.

He was a genius in adjusting his plans to the lay of the land, and also in taking towns, always sharing his soldiers' hardships. It was said at the time: 'A town besieged by Vauban was a town taken. A town defended by Vauban, was an impregnable town.' It was largely due to his work that France was able to expand and protect her boundaries.

He began his long career fighting for the Prince of Condé, in revolt against King Louis XIV. When Cardinal Mazarin persuaded him to fight for the king, he was twenty years old.

From 1655 to 1659, Vauban participated in 14 sieges and was wounded several times. Due to his experiences, Vauban reflected on the best method of attacking fortified places. At the same time, he began to formulate the best means of defence, using terrain and inter-locking works.

In 1667 he took part in the sieges of Tournai, Douai and Lille, which he took in just 9 days. The king gave him the job of building a citadel there which was to be called the queen of citadels (it's still there).

From 1668 onwards, Vauban fulfilled the duties of Commissioner General of Fortifications (a title he received in 1677). With the Franco-Dutch war of 1673, Vauban exhorted the king to reduce the number of strongholds and only keep the strongest which were not isolated in enemy territory. To protect the plain of Flanders, he constructed a double shield of 25 fortified towns including Lille, Dunkirk, Menin and Ypres in the first line and Gravelines, Saint-Omer, Arras and Douai in the second.

The successful siege of Maastricht in June 1673 gave him the opportunity to show off his new method of attack which he had developed in a treatise to the king called 'on the conduct of sieges', notably in the use of ricochet. This method saved many soldiers' and engineers' lives and forced Maastrich to surrender after only 13 days. Vauban criticised soldiers who exposed themselves pointlessly through bravado. The celebrated D'Artagnan himself died at this siege for just that reason. Vauban was instrumental in conquering la Franche-Comté, for his king.

Vauban's siege plan covered 14 phases. An attack, according to him, would never need longer than 46 days before the enemy surrendered. His never did take longer.

From 1679 to 1688, Vauban travelled throughout France working on coastal defences and those in the south, as well as supervising work on those in the north and east recently conquered by the king. In 1684, he took the formidable fortress of Luxemburg in less than a month. He continued to develop and inaugurate fortifications with multiple lines of defences dominated by defensive towers.

Becoming a lieutenant general in 1688, he travelled 4000 kilometre each year either laying siege to towns or repairing or constructing new fortifications.

He produced during his life numerous treatises on subjects as diverse as science, economy (he proposed a single European currency), agriculture and strategy. His plans for canals were taken up two hundred years after his death. In 1689 he asked Louis, in the name of liberty of conscience, to cease persecuting the Huguenots.

In 1694 he successfully defended Brittany against English attack and built many fortresses there. Created Marshal of France in 1703, the distinction crowned a career spent in the service of his king and country.

Vauban criss-crossed France endlessly, covering, it is estimated, about 180,000 kms (110,000) miles, which, given the roads of the time, and the means of transport, is truly astonishing.

Finally, worn out by the chronic bronchitis which had plagued him most of his life, and by the fatigue of a lifetime passed in travelling the execrable roads of the time and continual sieges, he died on the 30th March 1707 in Paris. His heart was buried in the church of Les Invalides in Paris among the greatest Marshals of France.

His work on offence for military engineers were translated into 15 languages, including Turkish and Russian, and were standards until the end of the nineteenth century.

He was, according to a biographer:

> A short man, who had a bellicose air, with a coarse or loutish look, nay brutal and ferocious. The appearance was deceptive. Never was a man more gentle, more compassionate, more obliging, nor more sparing of the lives of his troops, with a bravery which took all on himself and gave all to others.

Art

Brittany has long been, and remains, a favourite with artists. The school of Pont Aven (see the relevant day out), is the most famous example of this. The department, with its ever changing light, offers artists stunning natural beauty, from wide, white sand beaches and dramatic coastal cliffs to rolling green hills marked by ancient stone walls, thatch-roofed farmhouses, and brilliantly coloured flowers. There are some excellent art galleries in Brittany, for example in Quimper, Rennes and Nantes.

Terminology for the standing stones

Menhir: Single stone, standing by itself or in an alignment.
Cromlech: Standing stones (menhirs) in a circle.
Dolmen: Stones topped with others (for example, the capped pairs at Stonehenge).
Megalith: from the Greek, mega – big and lith, stone. Big stone.
Tumulus: A tomb covered with stone and/or earth. It can incorporate one of more dolmens.

Music

From historical accounts, it seems that the Celts were addicted to music, and so they still are. Brittany has one of the richest musical heritages in the world - expressed both in traditional styles and less traditional electrical arrangements and compositions.

Breton music, with a rich infusion of Irish tunes, can be heard all over the place at concerts and festivals (known as fez noz, 'night feasts'). Every year 600,000 Celts from all of the Celtic homelands descend on the Interceltic Festival in Lorient: but there are literally hundreds of musical festivals in Brittany each year – so it is highly likely that, if you visit between Easter and September, there will be some kind of festival being held in a town or village in the neighbourhood.

Kan ha diskan (call and response singing) is probably the most common type of Breton vocal music, especially when dance music is played. The lead singer, the kaner, sings a phrase, and the second singer, the diskaner sings the last few lines with the kaner, then repeats it alone until the same last few lines, when the kaner again joins in. The phrase's repetition is changed slightly in each execution. The **Chants de marins** are sea shanties, about shipwrecks, sailing and loss, often accompanied by the fiddle and accordion.

Since the Breton folk music revival, Scottish bagpipes and Irish harps have been added to the Breton repertoire, though Brittany has its own piping traditions which have been historically unbroken, as well as other instrumental traditions. The accordion, now the most popular Breton folk instrument, only arrived in large numbers in the country in about 1875.

Undoubtedly the most famous name in modern Breton music is **Alan Stivell**, who popularized the Celtic harp with a series of albums in the early 1970s. His harp was built by his father. Stivell's most important contribution to the Breton music scene, however, has probably been his importation of rock and other American styles, as well as the formation of the idea of a Breton traditional band.

The most famous band of Breton music is **Tri Yann** from Nantes who started playing in 1972 – their genre being progressive rock-folk-celto-medieval music ! Warning, the music is infectious.

Driving in France

Basics
In France, driving is on the right.
Distances are measured in kilometres. A kilometre is roughly 5/8ths of a mile. Ten kilometres is about 6 and a quarter miles. (There is an online distance calculator on our website www.enhancefrance.com)
The minimum age for driving in France is 18.

French policemen are strict. They can levy spot fines for infringements. Don't annoy them!

The use of seat belts is compulsory.

Children must be at least 10 years old to sit in the front. Under 10s must be seated in the rear and belted into an approved child seat (booster for non-babies). However, a very young child in an approved rear-facing safety seat can travel up front.

What to Take

Your driving license.

Holiday insurance for you and your family

An E111 form (EEC health cover) is needed from the U.K. (from post offices or 0800 555 777). From other English speaking countries, you must arrange your own.

Car insurance.

A warning triangle (compulsory after an accident or breakdown).

Those who come from countries where driving is on the left must put a converter on your headlights to cut glare.

Topping up with Petrol/Gas

Petrol (essence) sold at motorway service stations tends to be as expensive as in the UK (a good deal more expensive than the U.S!). From a hypermarket, it is about 10% cheaper. Savings on diesel can be even greater.

Main Roads

Brittany is served by a network of dual carriageways which are mostly near the coast. None of them are toll roads.

Speed Limits

In town 50 km/h (31 mph).

Single carriageways, out of town: 90 km/h - 80 when wet (56 and 50 mph).

Dual carriageways 110 km/h - 100 when wet (69 and 62 mph).

Motorways 130 km/h - 110 when wet (81 and 68 mph).

(when visibility is below 50m, speed limit is 50kmh everywhere).

Priorité a droite
Give way to traffic joining the road from the right. In the old days, even though you were driving along a more major road, you had to give way to any road joining it from the right. This does not apply on roundabouts any more, nor on any open roads of any significance, thank God. However, in built up areas you must give way to anyone coming out of a side turning on the right ....sometimes ....it depends on whether there is a white line across the side road and/or a sign telling them they must give way. Confused? That is always a possibility...

Flashing your lights
If you flash your lights in France, you are telling the other guy to get out of the way.

Traffic and Jams
A useful French site is www.autoroutes.fr As I say, useful, but about as quick as a traffic jam!

If you breakdown at a point where you disturb the flow of traffic, switch on your hazard warning lights and place a red warning triangle (which you should carry with you) 30m behind your vehicle.

Police should be informed of any **accident** which affects others or is serious. If a vehicle is damaged you should fill out "European Accident Statement" form, which comes with your green card (E111 - UK). Get it signed by the other driver. If you do not have a form, swap personal and insurance details with the other party.

Emergency Telephone Numbers
15 - Ambulance (SAMU = Service d'aide medicale urgent)
17 - Police
18 - Fire service (pompiers)
112 - all three services (like 999 in the U.K.)

Maps and Route Plotting

For an easily-handled folded map covering the whole of Brittany, we recommend the **IGN Carte Régionale R06** at 1/250,000. This is an excellent, clear map. It is not easily bought outside of France, but can be ordered from our website at www.enhancefrance.com If you intend to do more than one trip to France, we recommend that you take the **Michelin Motoring Atlas to France** (scale 1:200,000). This is readily available in shops, or via our website.

There are several excellent **online sites** for plotting a route, for example www.multimap.com, www.mappy.com and www.viamichelin.com. Multimap is also a good site for viewing and printing maps, with 8 levels of magnification, down to street level. Links to all of these can be found on our site, www.enhancefrance.com

Ferry Routes to France from Britain

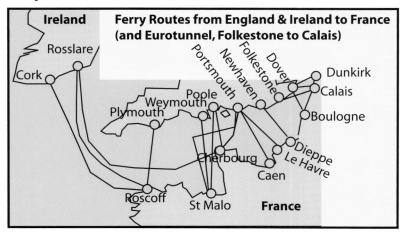

This map shows all of the ferry routes between Britain and Ireland, and France. To find out more, or book a passage, visit our web site, www.enhancefrance. There you will find what we believe to be the only complete list of ferry routes between Great Britain and Ireland, and France, on the web.

Index of Attractions

Our Website

www.enhancefrance has been built up over several years to provide useful information about France. With free translation and currency conversion tools, exchange homes, online maps (see above), ferries (see above), holiday cottages, hotels, insurance, lots about French property, the list keeps growing…
visit it to enhance your trip to France.

Other Books by Alan Biggins

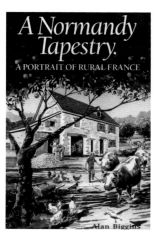

A Normandy Tapestry – a portrait of rural France

This deservedly popular book, now in its fifth printing, is an account of the life of an English family in Normandy. Alan, who moved to France to study French, supported himself by selling houses to British visitors. This took him behind the scenes of rural France. There are many amusing tales of family life and humorous incidents, such as bartering a bidet for calvados, being tutored in the ways of philosophy and septic tanks, and a meeting with the Six Potato Man.

ISBN 0-9523149-2-4. Available from bookshops, or via www.enhancefrance.com – **post free**.

Selling French Dreams

The sequel to the above. This tells more about life as an estate agent. Woven in is the tale of the Biggins family, the children at French school, Ann, the rock on which the family is anchored and Alan's tales of French rural life.
The book has a deeper significance in that it devotes a chapter to the pitfalls that have spoiled so many moves to France. It is essential reading for those considering buying French property or moving to France.

ISBN 0-9523149-5-9. Available from bookshops, or via www.enhancefrance.com – **post free**.

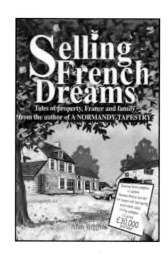